HUMAN RIGHTS IN THE BIBLE AND TALMUD

Haim H. Cohn

HUMAN RIGHTS
IN THE BIBLE
AND TALMUD

MOD Books   Tel-Aviv

HUMAN RIGHTS IN THE BIBLE AND TALMUD
by
HAIM H. COHN
Deputy President Emeritus,
Supreme Court of the State of Israel

Broadcast University Series
Galei Zahal — Tel Aviv University
Series Editor: Tirza Yuval

English translation by Shmuel Himelstein

English Series Editor: Shmuel Himelstein

ISBN 965-05-0563-6

Computerized Phototypesetting & Printing: Naidat Press Ltd.
Printed in Israel

MOD Books — P.O.B. 7103, Tel-Aviv 61070, ISRAEL

Contents

Preface 7

I.   Rights 9

II.   The Right to Life 18

III.   Equality and Difference 27

IV.   The Other Nations of the World 34

V.   Idolaters and the Members of Other Religions 42

VI.   The Stranger 49

VII.   Slavery 58

VIII.   Labor 71

IX.   Women 80

X.   Prophets: Freedom of Speech 90

XI.   Sages: Freedom of Opinion 98

XII.   The Right of Freedom 110

PREFACE

These lectures are meant for those young people who are concerned about human rights, but to whom the Biblical and Talmudic sources are unfamiliar — because they never learned them, because their teachers' attitudes soured them toward these sources, or because of their fear that this might smack of coercive Orthodoxy. Each educated person must know not only where he is going, but also where he comes from — and every Jew must have an idea of the glorious religious tradition of his people.

The choice of the topics and quotes was dictated by limitations of space. Most of the topics I chose appear to be irrelevant to our times, yet it is just in the approach taken by Jewish law to these topics that we find a message which is very much relevant. Almost all of the quotes in the Hebrew edition were given as they appear in the original, for one cannot truly appreciate the sayings of the Prophets and Sages except in their own words. The English translation has, accordingly, attempted to remain as close as possible to the original text of these quotations. I have refrained from giving references, in order not to make the reading of the text too cumbersome. All the quotes are from the Bible, the Talmud or the Midrash, unless stated otherwise. Whoever wishes to delve into the subject in greater depth will find sources in dictionaries and concordances. If I have succeeded, even if only in the case of a single reader, in arousing interest in our ancient sources or pride in them, I will feel amply rewarded.

I do not belong to those apologists who wish to justify everything that is found in our sources: if at the time of their giving the laws of the Torah were "just statutes and judgments," already in the Talmudic era, and all the more so in our time, the concept of "justice" and its demands had changed. The readers should therefore not be surprised if they find here discrimination which we would reject out of hand as untenable, and many laws which have become archaic. I have attempted to explain these, and to show how progressive they were in the special context of ancient societal life. The principles underlying these laws are the tradition upon which we are required to add and to build.

I offer these lectures, with great love, to my grandchildren and great-grandchildren, so that they may transmit the message to their children after them.

Haim H. Cohn

I.

Rights

It is difficult to speak about "human rights" in the Jewish legal tradition, for the simple reason that this tradition is a religious law, i.e., as it states about itself, it is a Divine law. Such a law, by its nature, does not grant rights but imposes obligations. The law that God gives is composed of "commandments"; the laws determine the obligations. The law that the Jews accepted at Mount Sinai, which was in the category of "we will observe and we will hear" (i.e., which was based on blind obedience), was and remains a law that only imposes obligations. The word "right" in its modern meaning of "that which is coming to me," is not to be found in either the Bible or the Talmud. I think that the first Jewish jurist who uses the term "right" in its modern-day legal meaning is Maimonides.

Nevertheless, when a legislator imposes an obligation or forbids one to perform a certain action, by implication he is also granting a right. From the prohibition of "you shall not murder," the implication is that a person has a "right" to live, and in order for his right to live not to be violated, one is forbidden to murder him. When I am told, "you shall not steal," it implies (even though this is not stated in the Torah) that my fellow has the "right" to own property. If I am commanded to return a lost object, it is clear that the thing I found does not belong to me but to the person who lost it, and that person has the "right" to that object.

It follows from this that we can only deduce "human rights" in religious and divine law by means of negation. The obligation, the commandment, is what creates a right alongside it, and recognizes that right.

In a theocracy, all the government is that of God; He is the absolute ruler, the only and supreme One. Even when there is a king, or a government led by a military or civilian leader or "the elders of the city," all are commanded to follow in the ways of and act in accordance with the commandments of God, His statutes and judgments. Therefore there is a special commandment for the king to write himself a Torah scroll. He does not receive a Torah scroll from his predecessor but must write his own scroll, so that he cannot claim that he does not know the statutes and the judgments in accordance with which he must act.

The entire divine law is directed at the individual, the individuum — and the king, too, is in this class. Whether the commandment is stated in the singular or the plural, the citizen is the addressee, and the entire nation is but the totality of all its citizens. And just as the obligations are those of the individual, so too are those rights which one can claim only the rights of the individual; this is as opposed to the modern citizen's rights, which are rights primarily *vis-a-vis* the state and *vis-a-vis* the different authorities: "freedom of opinion and speech" means that the government, the state, may not infringe on my right to speak or to think. So too am I granted, in Jewish religious law, the right to life and to freedom and all basic rights; but these are not rights *vis-a-vis* God but *vis-a-vis* man. *Vis-a-vis* God there are only obligations. Whatever I receive from Him is an act of mercy on His part, and I cannot demand any "right" from Him.

This does not mean that God is not involved in the rights which I have. If a person sinned toward me and I am unable or unwilling to sue him, there is God in the heavens, who observes both him and me, and who will see to it that the person will be punished and that justice will prevail, using His own ways. Thus we are taught that, "He who rendered an accounting with the people of the generation of the flood and the generation of the separation (i.e., the builders of the tower of Babel), will in the future render an accounting with one who does not keep his word." Even if you did not fulfill your obligation to keep your word, "the right" of the person who relied on your promise is preserved for him in heaven.

There are many "good and proper actions," in the words of Maimonides, many actions which it is very difficult to impose upon man — actions which are more ethical and moral than legal. Take, for example, the commandment of "you shall rise before the hoary head and honor the face of the old," or that of "you shall not place a stumbling block before the blind," or those actions which take place in privacy, of which no other person can be aware; it is in regard to these that the Torah often writes, "you shall fear your God" — do what you have been commanded to do and do not do that which you are forbidden to do, and do not fear any man or judge, but your God. "Should you say" — that is the language of the Midrash,

> that it is but good advice that I give you that you should rise for the hoary head and that this is discretionary on your part (i.e., that this is each person's individual concern, in accordance with his conscience and moral values), it therefore states, "you shall fear your God"; He looks and sees all, and do not deceive yourself into thinking that there is no eye that observes.

It therefore follows, in regard to the existence of the "rights" which stem from the commandments, that there is no difference whether a person can go to the courts and claim his right, or whether his obligation exists only as far as God is concerned. The person for whose benefit you do what you are commanded to do gains the benefit, and the right is granted him. The fact that your obligation is not to him but rather to God does not add or detract from the existence of the right.

It is customary to regard man's "basic rights" as being something with which he is born and which belong to him by the nature of his being. According to this viewpoint — that of "natural law" — there is no need, nor is there any reason, for laws that establish those rights or commandments or obligations which one can arrive at independently. Nevertheless, states pride themselves on those laws which guarantee their citizens their basic rights. Furthermore, there are also those who hold that, without a written and specific constitution, human rights are not guaranteed adequately. Be that

11

as it may, the Torah's "constitution" guarantees human rights well — not by establishing or describing them as such, but by imposing a holy obligation upon every person to honor them. One can possibly say that the Torah establishes human rights, not by positing rights but rather by rejecting actions which violate them; by defining the negation one defines the great affirmation.

Another aspect of Jewish law is that its provisions cover all areas of life and determine man's behavior, whether in regard to his Maker or in regard to his fellow-man, in every situation in which he may find himself. Our legal tradition does not differentiate between those commandments between man and his fellow, which, as mentioned, create "rights," and those ritual commandments which by their nature cannot and do not need to create "rights" — which God does not need. But those commandments between man and his fellow — and these are the topic which we will discuss — do not differentiate in judicial terms between moral or ethical commandments and legal commandments; the fact that a violation of moral or ethical norms carries no "sanction" in this world and no court can recognize a claim based on such a violation, does not detract from their status and importance as legal and religious norms. The prohibition against cheating and trickery in business is no greater, for example, than that of tale-bearing, even though the former can be enforced and can command compensation and the latter affords neither enforcement nor compensation; both violations are considered to be "sins," one of which commands punishment by man and the other only by God. And the "rights," too are equal: the right not to be the victim of slander is not lesser than the right not to be the victim of cheating.

In this context, there is special importance in the commandment of "you shall do that which is just and good" — and while this requirement is that one be "just and good in the eyes of the Lord," what is just and good in the eyes of God is honesty and uprightness in one's relations with people. A *midrash halakhah* (a *midrash* of *halakhic* content) explains the reason for the seeming redundancy of the words "just and good" as meaning just in the eyes of God and good in the eyes of man, as well as good in the eyes of God and just in the eyes of man. Not only the redundancy of the phraseology of the verse, but the redundancy of the phraseology in the midrash, teaches us that everything that is good is also just, and everything that is just is also good. Why, then, does the verse add the words, "in the eyes of God"? in order to explain that the standards of what is good and just are objective; it is not that "each shall do what is just in his own eyes," which the Bible understands to be despicable, but that people should do that which is just in the eyes of God and in the eyes of *all* mankind. This general and sweeping obligation, too, creates rights, these rights too being abstract in the sense that no earthly court can enforce them (except in terms of "beyond the measure of the law" — a term which we will be using extensively, and which implies going beyond the letter of the law). But regardless of how generalized and sweeping the obligation is, it is your right that I fulfill that obligation toward you; if I act toward you wickedly and deceitfully, I have violated one of your legal rights.

According to Nahmanides, the commandment of "you shall do that which is just and good" is meant to be the complement of all the other commandments in the Torah; one cannot list in advance all of man's behavior in all conditions and all the circumstances which may occur — and certainly not that of all people in all generations:

> The Torah cannot mention all of man's behavior with his neighbors and friends and all his dealings, and what is needed to ensure the welfare of mankind and of all states; but after having mentioned many of [the laws], such as "you shall not bear tales," "you shall not take vengeance or bear a grudge," "you shall not stand by the blood of your brother," "you shall not curse the deaf," "you shall rise before the hoary head," it repeats as a general principle that you shall do that which is good and just in every matter.

Thus we see that the obligations of a person to his fellow encompass all the possibilities and opportunities than can occur, and that a person's rights as far as his fellow are concerned are "human rights," whereby one must act toward him as a just and good person acts.

To us, though, the major aspect of "justice," as in the laws of other nations, is not the granting of rights but the forgoing of rights. Even if you have a legal right, such as the right to your property, you do "the just and the good" if, when the circumstances demand it, you do not insist on your rights. The appropriate circumstances vary from case to case, and are subject to a large extent to your generosity; the rule is that no right has the ability to *obligate* you to demand and enforce it. The right is, by its nature, permissive and not obligatory (except for rights which also entail obligations, such as the right to life), and one with a right may do with it "what he will." When R. Nehunia was asked why he had lived to a ripe old age, he answered: "I was yielding with my money" — to teach us that forgoing money through doing what is just and good is worthwhile in terms of the gains that accrue thereby. And this applies not only in regard to blessings from heaven such as old age, but also in regard to one's spiritual satisfaction and peace of conscience.

Just as the commandment of "doing what is just and good" refers to those with rights, it also refers to judges. Jethro's advice to Moses that he instruct the judges "of the actions that they are to do" is explained by the Sages of the Talmud: "'The actions' — this refers to the law; 'that they are to do' — that is beyond the measure of the law." Even if in accordance with the law a person possesses a recognized and valid right, one which is enforceable legally, the judges are nevertheless commanded on occasion to force the person with the right to yield either totally or partially. A person with a right who stubbornly insists on his complete right may cause injustice, even though "the law" is in accordance with him; but the judge will not lend his hand to the doing of an injustice, be the law as it is. The level of justice of this legal system is greater than that of any other: in modern law, "equity is subservient to the law," and the legislative body determines in advance the realm of the law and the realm and the nature of equity. The Talmud tells of a certain judge to whom workers came to sue for their wages. Their employer, the defendant, claimed that not only had they not worked, but they had broken his tools, and he demanded compensation for his loss. The judge ruled that the workers were entitled to their wages and were not obligated to pay damages for the tools. The defendant asked whether this was indeed the law. The judge answered him: "Indeed it is, as it states, 'That you may walk in the way of good men, and keep the paths of the righteous; for the upright will dwell in the land.'" One may assume that the workers were poor and hungry, and had not ruined their tools deliberately. "Equity," the enforcement of the person's yielding his right by law, enters into the realm of going "beyond the measure of the law," and overcomes the law itself. One might possibly even find support for this enforcement within the law itself, as it states: "You shall not harden your heart, nor shut your hand from your poor brother" — but that particular judge preferred to do what was "equitable" within the realm of "beyond the measure of the law."

Indeed, judgment beyond the measure of the law is not by any means limited to enforcing the yielding of a person's rights; it is no less important in enforcing a person's yielding on the carrying out of obligations toward him. The law is that a person is to be punished for his sins; but we are told that God, as it were, prays to Himself to behave "beyond the measure of the law." And there are occasions when the judge must pray to himself to find the courage in his soul to rule not in accordance with the law but beyond the measure of the law; it is much easier to follow in the path of the clear *halakhah* and to assume — as something which is self-evident — that the degree of justice in equity cannot in any event attain the degree of justice in the divine law, and thus for the judge not to place his feeling for justice above the provisions of the law. But "you shall do that which is good and just" is also a law of the Torah — and it is this which grants to judgments beyond the measure of the law their legal basis.

R. Yohanan states: "Jerusalem was destroyed only because [its judges] judged according to the law of the Torah." On this, the Talmud asks: Should they then have judged according to the laws of the non-Jews? Rather, the meaning is that Jerusalem was destroyed "because they based their judgments on the law of the Torah and did not go beyond the measure of the law." In other words, they implemented the law, but did not do that which was just and good.

15

And the converse is also true: a judge who has the courage not to enforce every right just because it is a legal right, and not to enforce every obligation just because it is a legal obligation, but rather does that which is just and good and equitable and proper in the case at hand, saves the world and society from destruction.

On the other hand, it is a major principle that every "right" is worthy of protection. A person who forgoes a certain right, or a judge who forces him to yield on it, does not infringe on the existence of the right itself; the exercise of the right can be waived in a certain matter and for a superior goal. Every right has a certain goal underlying it and a certain value in its enforcement; and morally — if not judicially as well — the value and the status and the protection of the right is in accordance with the nature of its goal and the extent of its value. Take, for example, the commandment of charity, the implication of which is that every person has the right to his sustenance: there is no loftier goal than "that there will be no poor person among you," and there is no greater and more essential value than "your brother will live with you." Indeed, this right is enshrined in the Torah in the laws of fallen stalks of wheat that must be left for the poor, grain forgotten in the field which may not be retrieved, the corner of the field that must be left unharvested, and the poor man's tithe. So too is there the prohibition against taking interest and against not paying wages on time; the prohibition against hardening one's heart and shutting one's hand, and the commandment to "surely open your hand to him," "to support him," etc. In the words of Maimonides:

> Whatever the poor person lacks, you are required to give him. If he has no garment, one clothes him; if he has no household utensils, one buys these for him; if he has no wife, one marries him off; and if it is a woman, one marries her off to a man — as it states "that which he lacks, which he is missing."

But with all the importance and the essential nature of the right, a person can say: "I don't want to marry that woman"; and it is even "a saintly quality" "to make one's Sabbath a weekday," i.e., to eat simple weekday fare, "and not to have to come to people" for one's support. A basic right, like the ultimate right of rights, is that of a person to yield on his rights; but just as a person is not permitted to use his right if he thereby denies or endangers the right of his fellow, so is a person forbidden to yield on his right when he thereby denies or endangers a superior right of his own, such as the right to life. Again, as Maimonides puts it:

> Whoever needs to take (charity) and does not do so, and cannot live unless he takes it, such as a person who is old or sick or is suffering, and coarsens his mind and does not take it, sheds blood thereby and is worthy of death.

If there is an obligation for one who has a certain right to use that right, it is like a right of "the One to whom all souls belong," but who is, of course, above all rights.

II.

The Right to Life

As mentioned above, the right to life stems from the prohibition against killing. Cain, who killed Abel, not only committed a grave wrong to the murdered man — although nothing is written about that wrong — but we are told that the voice of the blood of Abel cried out *to God* from the earth. The wrong of murder is against God; and indeed, the first law, given immediately after the flood — and consequently also the first prohibition in the Torah — is "he who sheds the blood of man, by man shall his blood be shed." In that same verse we also find the answer why God does not tolerate the shedding of blood, "for in the image of God He created man." He who sheds the blood of man kills the image of God.

Thus did R. Akiva expound: Whoever sheds blood is considered as if he "decreased the image," as if he has detracted from God Himself. So too do we find that the shedding of blood brings about a defilement of the holy land: "The land cannot be cleansed of the blood that is shed on it but by the blood of him that shed it. Do not therefore defile the land which you will inhabit." Do not defile it by shedding blood.

The punishment of one who sheds the blood of man is that his blood is shed. A life for a life is the commandment of God, to whom belong all souls. He can do with them as He wishes; just as He Himself can kill, so too can He command us to kill those who have killed. In the Torah, there are many major sins whose punishment is, "He shall surely be put to death." There are thus circumstances

18

when we can become emissaries, as it were, of God, who generally takes life just as He gives it; for there are times when He commands us to kill in His place.

How far this prohibition against killing goes can be seen from the law of the *eglah arufah* — the "heifer whose neck is broken." Where a murdered person's body is found and his murderer is unknown, the elders and judges and priests of the town where the body was found must come and wash their hands "over the heifer whose neck is broken in the valley," and all must proclaim: "Our hands did not spill the blood and our eyes did not see." As long as the murderer goes about free and has not been punished, we have not fulfilled God's commandment and the land remains defiled; thus, in lieu of the punishment of the murderer, another "atonement" is called for.

When a person's life is taken, either through murder or killing, there is intervention in the Divine privilege of taking life. Only God may kill. A person is forbidden to kill unless commanded to do so by God.

As far as every other person is concerned, I have the right to live, while as far as God is concerned, I do not have that right. He can kill me at any moment, either through disease or by any other means. If He does so, I have no right to complain to Him, for He has deprived me of that which He gave me, the right to live. But although I have the right to live as far as every other person is concerned, I cannot realize that right to life if a person kills me; just as I cannot realize it when a court is required to kill me at God's command.

In the Bible, we find the survival of the concept of the redeemer of blood, who has the instinctive human reaction of revenge. If a person close to me — my father, my mother or my child — is killed, it is natural that I will want to kill the killer. The lust for revenge within man was placed within a legal framework: the redeemer of blood cannot kill the murderer unless the person was killed through negligence. As a bulwark against the utilization of this right, the Torah established cities of refuge. In these, a person who had killed another through negligence could find sanctuary from the redeemer of blood who pursued him. We will yet discuss the nature of the cities of refuge in another context.

If this is the law where a person killed another through negligence, logic would dictate that the same law should apply in the case of premeditated murder. But the law is that the redeemer of blood is not permitted to kill the murderer if a court has ruled that this man is guilty, and that what he did was premeditated (and we will not elaborate here on the proof needed for this). The reason for this is that a person who kills by premeditation has sinned, first of all, against God, and it is not the redeemer of blood but the court which is authorized to kill him. As far as the lust of the redeemer of blood for vengeance is concerned, the one who killed through negligence deserves protection in that he is not entirely guilty. As opposed to this, the court which implements the law requiring a premeditated murderer to be killed offers no possibility for the murderer to obtain refuge.

All signs indicate that the Sages of the Talmud were not at ease with the divine command to kill a murderer, or to kill other sinners who had committed sins whose punishment is death. What did they do in order to prevent such executions, when the Torah commanded, "He shall surely be put to death"?

In addition to the specific Torah requirement of two witnesses who actually saw the act being carried out, without which one cannot prove the guilt of the sinner, they added a requirement for two more witnesses. The latter had to testify that before the act had been committed they had warned the person and told him: "Know that what you are about to do is forbidden by Torah law, and know that if you do it, you will be sentenced to death." Some say that even that was insufficient, and that the witnesses had to specify in advance to the person exactly which death penalty he would face if he carried out the action; whether by stoning, the sword, burning or strangling. After the person had been told clearly that what he was about to do was forbidden and what the penalty would be if he nevertheless carried out the action, he no longer could maintain that he had killed without knowing that such an action was forbidden, or that he had been unaware of the punishment for such an action. But even this was not sufficient. The person would have to reply to the two warning witnesses: "You are my witnesses that I know the law; I know that I am forbidden to kill, and nevertheless and in spite of this I will kill." If he did not make this clear statement, the warning itself was valueless, and no death penalty could be imposed by the courts. On the other hand, if after the warning the person made a clear declaration that he was aware of the sin and of its punishment, he in essence "permitted himself to be killed." However, if a person was told that one is forbidden to kill and that if he killed a certain individual he himself would be killed by the sword, he would probably refrain from carrying out his intention; either because his rage would have subsided by then, or because he would wait to carry out the action after the witnesses had left — and then the law is that there would be the need for new warning witnesses and witnesses to the act itself.

It thus appears that the need for witnesses to warn the person about to commit a crime, in addition to witnesses to the crime itself, totally abolished the death penalty for all practical purposes. And indeed, we have the famous mishnah which quotes R. Akiva and R. Tarfon: "Had we been in the Sanhedrin (the highest Jewish court during Second Temple times and for a few centuries thereafter), no person would ever have been put to death," and which states further that a Sanhedrin responsible for one execution in seven years — and some say one in seventy years — "is called injurious," as if the judges are injuring men's lives. As opposed to these, we have the view of R. Simeon b. Gamaliel, who states: "They are increasing the number of murderers in Israel." If one does not kill murderers, if one does not punish them in accordance with the law, there will be nothing to deter others from killing. He was the criminologist in the group, whereas R. Akiva and R. Tarfon were the humanists.

In the Talmud, the Sages debate the issue and ask how it is possible not to execute a person if he has indeed carried out an act whose penalty is death, if the law permits his execution. The answer is that when they come to examine the witnesses thoroughly, they will ask them questions that will almost certainly involve them in contradictions, and when the witnesses contradict one another, their testimony will be annulled and there will be no recourse but to free the accused.

We can thus see to what lengths the Sages of the Talmud went in order to make it difficult to impose the death penalty — even by the courts, and even when the Torah specified clearly that the sinner was to be put to death. All deliberative means were permissible, as long as the Sages did not intervene in the divine privilege, in God's monopoly, and did not kill a person.

Even more than this, one must be amazed and astounded at what the Sages of the Talmud did in regard to the punishment of *karet*. *Karet* is a death penalty imposed by God, not by a mortal court. In the Torah we are told, "the soul will be cut off (*ve-nikhreta* in Hebrew, i.e., it will suffer *karet*) from the midst of its people," which the Sages interpreted to mean that God chooses the time that He wishes and the means that He wishes to cut off the soul from the midst of its people, i.e., to end the sinner's life. The Sages of the Talmud regarded this threat of *karet* as not being in keeping with what we would refer to today as human rights. In essence, if I have committed a sin the punishment for which is *karet*, I have to live under a perpetual threat of a divine punishment, where God will choose the time and the method to punish me, the means by which this will occur, today or next week or thereafter, and in a way that I cannot foretell in advance, possibly even in the most cruel and terrible way, and where I am liable to be punished for something that I may have done years ago, and this is true even if in the interim I became a good and just man. It is true that God's mercy is infinite, but who knows what lies in wait for me and whether God will exert His mercy in my particular case, or whether He will carry out His threat that my soul will be cut out from the midst of the nation.

The Sages saw that, in reality, this too was a death penalty, and possibly an even more cruel one, because it was unexpected and undefined, and that it was liable to cause constant and unbearable fear. They therefore ruled that a person who deserves *karet* is to receive lashes — i.e., 39 lashes — and once he has received these lashes, he has received his punishment and his soul will no longer be cut off from the midst of his people; the one who received lashes will live and not die. His right to life is preserved for him, and he has been saved, so to speak, from God's hands before He has managed to harm him. And if one asks: How can we be sure that God indeed will tolerate the substitution of lashes for *karet*? Could He not be laughing in His heavens and saying, as it were: "They have given him 39 lashes, but I will send My *karet* at My time and as I wish"? The Sages attempt to solve this problem. One says: There is a rule, and God, of course, knows the major rules, that a person is not punished twice for the same sin; we have already punished him with 39 lashes, he has already suffered them, and God will not punish him a second time. After all, He is a God of justice, He is a God of mercy, "Will the Judge of all the earth not do justice?" Another says: Every punishment that you impose on a person has an element of atonement — especially if the person who was punished repented, regretted his actions, and received lashes. When a person has atoned for his sins, there is nothing left for which to punish him. He is no longer subject to *karet*, for the sin no longer exists. The man has already repented, he has already received his punishment, he has already atoned, and the case is now closed.

But R. Isaac, one of the great jurists of the Talmudic Sages, disagrees with his colleagues and says: *Karet* is better and less cruel than lashes; when we speak of *karet*, every sinner has the hope in his heart that God may be merciful and may not exact the punishment; man is by nature hopeful. This is not the case with lashes, whose pain is immediate, and whose suffering is real. It is thus better to leave the *karet* in effect and to leave the sinner to God's mercies, rather than to have the courts impose a punishment that the Torah never authorized them to.

But the very idea that one must try to preserve man's life, even if his death might come from Heaven — that it is better to decree a punishment of lashes, rather than have the person punished by being put to death, whether by man or by God — proves to what extent the Sages went in preserving the right to life. And they succeeded in their task, not only for those whom the mortal courts were commanded to kill, but even for those whose death penalty was guaranteed them by Heaven.

The third of the Ten Commandments states: "You shall not bear the name of the Lord your God in vain, for the Lord will not hold blameless he who bears His name in vain." If a person bears God's name in vain, if he swears falsely in God's name, his sin is so great that he cannot become "blameless" for that sin. The Sages investigated and found that it states there, "The Lord will not hold blameless he who bears His name in vain." God will not hold him blameless, but we can hold him blameless. If He is unwilling to forgive a false oath in His name, we will forgive the person. We, the court of flesh and blood, will take upon ourselves the freedom to save a major sinner from a death sentence and will leave him alive. And we can learn from this that if God states clearly that *He* will not hold blameless, we have His assent for us to hold the person blameless.

There is a famous law that whatever the commandments and prohibitions are in the Torah, underlying them we find the principle of "He will live by them and not die by them": whatever God commanded us to do, must only be done provided and subject to the fact that we are able to live, and that observing the commandments will not place our lives in jeopardy. Jeopardy to human life takes precedence over everything. There are only three sins for which one must allow himself to be killed rather than violate them — the shedding of blood, idolatry and sexual immorality. But even in these three the law of allowing oneself to be killed rather than violating the law only applies if one is forced to commit these sins in public, before ten or more people, or else he will be killed. Only in such circumstances must a person allow himself to be killed and not violate the law, the reason for this being that allowing oneself to be killed in such circumstances is a public sanctification of God's name. In one's own private premises, he is even permitted to commit sexual immorality or idolatry rather than be killed. I am unsure whether this applies to the shedding of blood as well; a person cannot know if "his blood is more red than that of another," as the Talmud puts it, i.e., one cannot tell whose life is more important. In such a case, rather than one's remaining alive himself by killing another, it is better that the other remain alive.

There is a dispute among the early rabbinic sages as to what takes precedence: one's own life or that of one's fellow. The hypothetical question posed is as follows: suppose you and another person are in the desert. You have only enough water with you to keep you alive, while your fellow has none. Should you share the water with your fellow, both will die. R. Akiva says: "'Your brother will live *with you*' — this teaches that your life takes precedence over that of your fellow." If you have a choice whether to remain alive yourself or to keep your fellow alive, it is better that you remain alive, even if it means your fellow will die. But Ben Petura says: "It is not fitting for you to remain alive and to see the death of your fellow." It is better that you not allow your fellow to die, even if you yourself will die, and do not walk about your entire life with the terrible feeling that it was you, through remaining alive, that caused your fellow to die. In terms of the right to remain alive, R. Akiva's view reflects the natural human survival instinct — and he may have regarded it as a superhuman demand to prefer one's fellow's life over one's own. As opposed to this, Ben Petura holds that a moral person will overcome his natural lusts, and will always find the strength in himself to attribute greater importance to another's life — or at least the same importance to the other's life — than to his own life. And it was not for naught that R. Akiva needed a specific verse in the Torah, "Your brother will live with you," upon which to base himself, as opposed to Ben Petura, who saw no need for support from one verse or another, and who may even have held that the simple meaning of "Your brother will live with you" is that both of you are to live as long as possible, and not that one should die at the expense of his fellow.

This, too, is based on human rights: that when you demand a certain right for yourself, you must grant that same right to others. You cannot use your right — and the right to life is included in this — at the expense of the denial of that right to others.

From this we see the right — or the obligation — to defend oneself: if a person comes to kill you, you are permitted to take preemptive measures and kill him. By the same token, you are commanded to rescue a person who is being pursued from the hands of his pursuer, "even at the expense of killing the pursuer." And this law applies even if the pursuer is not pursuing the person with murder in mind, but rape. It is true that if a person is able to rescue someone who is being pursued by other means than killing the pursuer and instead does so by killing the pursuer, he is considered to be a murderer; killing the pursuer is only permitted as a last resort. But "You shall not stand by the blood of your brother," which means that one must rescue him from danger, is another expression of the holiness of the life of everyone else. And if you are not permitted to stand by the blood of your brother, this is all the more true for your own blood.

III.

Equality and Difference

The following is from the first paragraph of the Universal Declaration by the United Nations on human rights: "All human beings are born free and equal in dignity and rights and honor." The equality between people, and the declaration that all people were born free and equal, are not the inventions of the authors of this declaration; their basis, as with that of the vast majority of basic human rights, lies in Jewish sources.

The Bible teaches that God created man in His image and likeness, "in the image of God He created him, male and female He created them." Every person was created in the image of God, and all people are equal in this respect. The one and only difference between them is mentioned in that verse itself, and that is the difference between male and female. But even the difference between the sexes is only mentioned there to stress the equality between them: just as the male was created in the image of God, so too was the female created in His image. It is not that God has a sex (or at least, there is no proof that He has a sex), but the fact that there is a physical and physiological difference between the male and the female is not enough to affect the personal, ethical and legal equality between them. This is a basic principle: because every person was created in God's image, every person is equal to every other, and no person has the right to say to his fellow, "I am greater than you; my blood is redder than yours."

Two sages argued over the "basic principle" of the Torah. R.

27

Akiva says, the basic principle of the Torah is, "You shall love your neighbor as yourself"; Ben Azzai, on the other hand, who was his contemporary and his student, differs and says that the basic principle of the Torah is "This is the book of the generations of man, on the day that God created man, in the image of God He created him, male and female He created them." What is the difference between R. Akiva and Ben Azzai? The former says that it is impossible to demand that one must love every person equally; one cannot "love" a person who is a stranger, whom one is not even capable of knowing or understanding. It is enough if one loves his neighbor, the one who is close to him, who belongs to his family, his tribe, his nation. Ben Azzai, on the other hand, says every person was born in the image of God: just as one must love God, so must one treat all people equally. That is the basic principle of the entire Torah. We have learned from our long experience that it may even be harder to love those who are close to us than those who are far from us. Those that we bump into each day and every hour are also the ones with whom we clash each day and every hour, or — at the least — we are liable to bump into them and quarrel with them. The greatest hate that judges confront is that between spouses or between heirs. The further the distance between people, the less the hatred between them; and even if there may not be any great "love" for those who are far away, there can and must at least be a feeling of respect for them.

But that is a psychological difficulty, which has nothing to do with the meaning of the Bible. What is important to us is that the fundamental equality between people — that we must treat each of them as having been created in the image of God — is a basic principle upon which the entire Torah of Israel is based.

This basic principle remains a moral, ethical and philosophical one. No special judicial conclusions stem from it or have been based on it. Only a very marginal matter has emerged from this principle, which is very typical of the pragmatic and practical approach of Jewish law. There is a law that a person must wash his face, his hands and his feet each day, because he was created in the image of God. In this regard, they tell a story about Hillel the Elder. Once, when his students asked him, "Where are you going?" He answered, "To perform a commandment." "What commandment?" they persisted. "To wash in the bathhouse," he responded. They said to him, "And is that then a commandment?" He replied to them:

> Yes. We know that the beautiful statues of kings that are placed in the theaters and circuses have a person who job it is to clean and wash them and to bring food to them, and the person who takes care of these statues is considered to be one of the great men in the kingdom. It follows that I, who was created in [God's] image and likeness, as it states, "In the image of God He created man," must all the more be clean.

And as every person was created in the image of God, man must follow in His ways, as it states in the Torah, "You shall go in His ways." If you should then ask, how can a person go in the ways of God? the Sages responded: As man was created in God's image and likeness, he must try to emulate God, in behavior rather than in terms of externals. Just as God clothes the naked, so must you clothe the naked; just as He cheers the sick, so must you cheer the sick; just as He comforts the mourners, so must you comfort the mourners; just as He is compassionate and merciful, so must you be compassionate and merciful. This is seen in the Torah: "You shall be holy, because I the Lord your God am holy": it is My holiness that imparts the holiness that is imposed on you.

There are those Jewish authorities who state that to say that God is "compassionate and merciful, long-suffering and filled with mercy" is "audacity toward Him": One who says that God has qualities such as these, is, as it were, measuring Him using human measurements, whereas God is beyond any description. The assumption is that certain qualities were attributed to God in order to make them human qualities, worthy of emulation. Just as He is compassionate, so are you to be compassionate. There is nothing more lofty than compassion, for God too is compassionate, and you must strive to resemble Him. The unique "paternal concern" of God which is mentioned in the Torah — as, for example, that God loves orphans, widows and strangers — is only meant to stress that it is just those people whom one perhaps does not naturally love and whom one may even despise — the weak and the persecuted and the oppressed, who by man's nature he oppresses and hates and scorns — that God loves with a divine "love," and this must serve as an example of how one must act.

The most beautiful — and possibly the most important — conclusion reached in Jewish law from the equality of human beings and their creation in God's image, is to be found in a mishnah in Tractate *Sanhedrin*. There we are told that the court must threaten the witnesses, before they testify, to be sure that they do not lie. And how does one threaten witnesses in capital punishment cases? First one warns them that they will be subject to a searching cross-examination. Afterwards, it is explained to them that "in torts — a person pays money and atones thereby; in capital cases, his blood and that of his descendants, until the end of the world, depends upon [the witness' testimony]." Thus, it is pointed out to the witnesses, we are told about Cain who killed Abel: "The voice of your brother's blood cries out to Me from the earth." It does not state *dam ahikha* — "the blood of your brother," but the plural form, *demei ahikha* — "the *bloods* of your brother" — his blood and that of his descendants after him. The judges must also add the following admonition to the witnesses:

> The reason that Adam was created alone is to teach you that whoever destroys a single human being is considered by the Bible as if he had destroyed the entire world; and whoever keeps a single human alive is considered by the Bible as if he had kept the entire world alive.

In other words, if you lie in your testimony and as a result of your testimony a person is condemned to death, you have not only killed a single individual, but are considered to have caused the destruction of a complete world. The judges add a further explanation for why Adam was created alone:

> That there should be peace among mankind, that no person should say to his fellow: "My father is greater than your father"; and (further), to show the greatness of God, for if a person mints a number of coins using a single die, all resemble

one another; yet when God placed His seal on every person using the die of Adam, none resembles his fellow. Therefore, every person must say: "The world was created for my sake." The world was created for my life, in honor of me, for my existence; for me as much as for you, and for us as for all of mankind.

It follows from this that the entire world was created for the individual, for each single unique person. As much as people differ from one another, all are equal in that each is different from his fellow: each with his character, his views, his beliefs, his physiognomy, his tendencies and his heredity. The very fact that what we all have in common is our differences from one another is what creates the equality between us: and it is these differences which determine the individuality of each person. Thus it is perfectly logical that the world was created for each person individually. In addition to the fact that all human beings are equal in having been born in the image of God, there exists what is referred to today as "pluralism" between people: it is good that each one differs from his fellow, and each one has the right to develop his unique talents and character, or those which he chooses to.

As mentioned, the mishnah establishes these basic principles of equality and of the differences between people specifically in regard to capital cases. If a person is on trial and a witness by false testimony causes him to be put to death, his blood and that of his descendants is "blamed" on the witness.

When someone is convicted and is taken out to be executed, R. Meir says: "When a person is in distress, what does the Divine Presence say?" In other words, what is God's reaction to the distress of this criminal who was justly convicted? He "is distressed at the blood of the wicked that was spilled; how much the more for that of the righteous."

So important is human life in God's eyes, that even when His commandments have been obeyed and the person is executed in accordance with Torah law, even then — of this R. Meir is sure — God, as it were, sits and is distressed at the blood which was spilled. And we have already seen to what extent the Sages went to save God

31

this distress and to prevent a person from being executed. How much more is God distressed at the blood of a righteous person who was killed either deliberately or through negligence, and who did not deserve the death penalty in accordance with the law. But the world was created for all people, the righteous and the wicked, and as far as God, Creator of the world is concerned, there is no difference as to whose life was cut off — that of a righteous person or a wicked one, a Jew or a non-Jew, a white or a black.

And that same R. Meir, who is so familiar with God's thoughts, gives us an analogy:

> What does this resemble? (It resembles) two brothers in a single city, one of whom was appointed king while the other became a brigand. The king then issued orders and they hanged the brigand. Whoever saw the body, said, "The king has been hanged!" The king thereupon ordered that the body be taken down.

Rashi explains that "this case involved two identical twins; man, too, is made in the image of God." We are all identical twins who were created in the image of God: every king has a brother who is a criminal, and every criminal has a brother who is a king.

The Talmud tells of a man who came to Rabbah (according to another version, it was Rava) and asked him what to do:

> "The ruler of the city has commanded me to kill a certain person, and if not he will kill me." He (Rabbah) said to him: "Let him kill you, but you may not kill! Who says that your blood is any redder? Maybe the other man's blood is redder!"

This, as we saw, is also the approach of Ben Petura, who ruled that it is better for a person to die himself rather than see the death of his fellow. We find a similar idea in the Jerusalem Talmud:

> If a caravan of people was told by non-Jews, "Give us one of you and we will kill him — and if not, we will kill all," it is better that all be killed, and that they not hand over a single person to be killed.

The reason is because the lives of all are equal. Not only that: the life of any individual is equal to the lives of the entire group. The words of the prophet, "Have we not all one father? has not one God created us? why do we deal treacherously every man against his brother?" sum up well the belief in equality and the obligations stemming from it: any lording by one person over another, any claim to a superior racial stock or of special uniqueness, is nothing but "dealing treacherously" with one's fellow-man. At least in potential, all people are born equal and remain equal, and all together are "but a little lower than the angels," having been crowned with glory and honor.

IV.

The Other Nations of the World

Just as the sanctity of the life of one's fellow does not taken precedence over one's right of defense and the commandment to save others, the sanctity of the equality of all people does not take precedence over the natural hatred for enemies and oppressors. The Christian view (only on the theoretical level), whereby one must love his enemy, is superhuman, and the comment has indeed been made that this represents the banishing of nature from morals. The Torah is satisfied with a less stringent commandment, although it is sufficiently stringent: "If you meet your enemy's ox or his ass going astray, you shall surely bring it back to him again. If you see the ass of him that hates you lying under his burden, and would abstain from helping him, you shall surely help with him." In other words, do not enrich yourself unjustly, even at the expense of an enemy or one who hates you.

This is not true for hostile nations. At first you must offer your enemy peace, and "if he does not make peace with you and makes war against you" and you emerge victorious, you are commanded to kill the males, and "the women, children and cattle and everything that there is in the city, all of its booty, you may take for yourself." Indeed, the Bible is replete with tales of how various Jewish leaders or monarchs fulfilled this commandment (or invitation) to the best of their ability. All signs indicate there was no other way for the nation to survive in those days. But we can learn from this that we are not to embark on any war unless we have first appealed to our enemies for peace.

This does not apply where enemies attack without warning. That is what happened to us when we left Egypt, when Amalek swooped down upon us from the rear, and we were "weary and exhausted," and "not yet fearing God." From then on, Amalek has remained the prototype of the cruel, inhuman enemy, and in order to remind ourselves of how God rescued us from Amalek's clutches, we are commanded to remember "that which Amalek did to you," and not to forget it. Yet, as God promised that "I will surely destroy the memory of Amalek underneath the heavens," we too are commanded to say: "Destroy the memory of Amalek under the heavens." On the one hand, we are required to remember Amalek, while on the other we are required to blot out his memory. King Saul was punished grievously when in his battle against Amalek he left over a remnant and did not utterly destroy the nation. King Hezekiah of Judea finally completed the task and destroyed "the surviving remnant of Amalek" — thus the commandment to destroy Amalek no longer exists. But the commandment to remember still remains. The Midrash tells us that the Children of Israel came to God and said to Him: "We are mortals, we live only for a time, while You live and exist for all eternity. And yet You tell us, 'Remember'?" God told them: "My children, all you have to do is to read the section on Amalek in the Torah each year, and I will consider it as if you have destroyed his name from the world." Thus we see that even perpetual "remembrance" is beyond man's ability — and by reading the section of the Torah on "remembering" Amalek we fulfill not only the obligation to "remember," but also the obligation to "destroy" him, even if only symbolically.

It is customary among us to use the word "Amalek" to describe all those nations that persecuted and tortured and burned and killed us throughout the generations; and we have accepted the obligation to remember and not forget them. If this is true for Amalek, how much more true is it for the Inquisition and the pogroms and the Holocaust.

But Amalek was not the only nation that fought us when we left Egypt. The Egyptians themselves oppressed and tortured us and killed our children, and indeed they were punished, with their firstborn killed and their army drowned in the sea. Yet, not only are we not commanded to destroy their name from beneath the heavens, but we are commanded: "You shall not abhor an Egyptian, because you were a stranger in his land." As cruel as they were to us, forcing us to engage in conditions of slave labor, we are not permitted to hold a grudge against them, because we lived in their land. And the same is true for the Edomite, who waged a fierce war against us: "You shall not abhor an Edomite, because he is your brother." And why is the Edomite "your brother"? because Edom is Esau, the brother of our father Jacob. On the other hand, because the Edomites and Moabites "did not greet you with bread and water on the way when you left Egypt," we are told that "you shall not seek their welfare and good all your days for ever." It is possible that one is not allowed to abhor them, but there is no cause to befriend them and "to cleave to them."

The Mishnah tells about an Ammonite convert who came to the Sages and asked them: "May I come among the congregation?" The Torah states, "An Ammonite and a Moabite may not come in the congregation of the Lord, even the tenth generation of them shall not come in the congregation of the Lord for ever." Rabban Gamaliel said: "You are forbidden." R' Joshua said: "You are permitted. Are the Ammonites and Moabites then in their (original) places? When Sennacherib king of Assyria ascended, he mixed together the nations," and we have no idea who belongs to what original nation. In the end, we are told, "they permitted him to come in the congregation." This implies that the prohibition of "You shall not seek their welfare and good" no longer applies — there is no longer any way of ascertaining to whom it applies. We are also told, in regard to the "Seven Nations" of ancient Canaan, that "you shall utterly destroy them," but, Maimonides adds, "their memory has already been lost." These nations, too, were mixed with others, and one cannot identify their members.

The Seven Nations and the Ammonites and the Moabites and the Egyptians, are the only ones with whom the Torah forbids intermarriage, but the prohibition of the Egyptians applies only to

36

the third generation, while the prohibition of the Ammonites and Moabites is evidently limited to the tenth generation. An eternal prohibition applies only to the Seven Nations — and the reason is only the fear that "their daughters will go awhoring after their gods, and make your sons go awhoring after their gods," or, in other words, the danger of idolatry. This danger probably existed as far as all the nations of the ancient world were concerned; nevertheless, the eternal prohibition only applied to the Seven Nations.

Ruth the Moabitess was accepted into "the congregation of the Lord" with open arms, and no attempt was made to calculate whether she was beyond "the tenth generation," nor was there anyone that questioned her legitimacy as was done with the Ammonite convert. Not only that, but Boaz went out of his way to seek "her welfare and good" — and we have no record of the elders in the gate protesting against his behavior. Even before she left her own god and followed Naomi's God, when she was still an idolater, Khilion the son of Elimelekh, of Bethlehem Judea, married her. We will still return to the question of her conversion; here we will merely indicate that Ruth the Moabitess was chosen to be the maternal ancestor of King David, and it has been prophesied to us that the Messiah, too, will stem from her.

There are many cases of intermarriage in the Bible, even without conversion. Among his other wives, King David took Maachah, daughter of the king of Geshur. David's son, Solomon, went even further and took an Ammonitess, one of the Ammonite royalty; the mother of Rehoboam was Na'amah the Ammonitess. In general, it is common knowledge that Solomon had many foreign wives; but when the prophets came to him with complaints about his exaggerated polygamous tendency, they never blamed him for taking non-Jewish women.

The first time firm opposition was expressed was at the time of Ezra and Nehemiah. According to Ezra, the wives that "the priests and the Levites," "the ministers and the assistants," "the singers and the gatekeepers," and all "of the Israelite people" took were of the daughters of "the Canaanite, the Hittite, the Perizite, the Jebusite, the Ammonite, the Moabite, the Egyptian and the

Emorite" — all of them idolaters, all of them women of "the detested nations." From the list at the end of Ezra, we see that, in spite of all the threats of the seizure of property and excommunication, this only brought about 113 husbands divorcing their non-Jewish wives; and indeed there was the need of the "covenant" of Nehemiah, to which all the leaders of the nation agreed, to establish a prohibition "that we will not give our daughters to the other nations of the land and we will not take their daughters for our sons" — and "the nations of the land" are nothing but those "nations of abominations."

Scholars are divided about the motivation of Ezra and Nehemiah: there are those who say that they wanted to prevent these women from enticing their sons into idolatry, and therefore "it would be done in accordance with the Torah" if they would force the husbands to divorce their non-Jewish wives. Others say that their intention was to purify "the holy seed" of foreign admixtures. Maimonides regards the decree of the "covenant" as a prohibition against intermarrying with "all the nations." In the Talmud, though, we find that only in the days of Hillel and Shammai, i.e., four hundred years later, did they "decree about the daughters" of all the other nations (i.e., forbidding intermarriage), and not necessarily because of the reason of the purity of the race, but "because of another matter" — and that, evidently, was the fear of idolatry. The Mishnah already mentions the "foreigner" among the list of women one is forbidden to marry.

As to the purity of the "race," Moses took a Cushite woman. This was not accepted by the members of the family: his brother and sister spoke out against "the Cushite woman that he took, because he took a Cushite woman." Had this marriage been opposed by God, He would presumably have been angry at Moses (as had occurred earlier); but not only did He not find any blemish in the Cushite woman, but He became angry at Aaron and Miriam for daring to speak out against Moses. He punished Miriam in the location where she had sinned: in the color of her skin; "and behold Miriam was leprous as snow." She appeared "like a dead person," as if "half her flesh" had been eaten. Only after Moses (and possibly his Cushite wife as well) pleaded to God on her behalf, was Miriam cured of her leprosy. The aggadists made valiant attempts to explain the word "Cushite" as a synonym for beautiful, but had Moses taken a beautiful woman, even in addition to his Midianite wife Zipporah, no one would have come with complaints against him. The fact that "he took a Cushite woman" was what brought these base feelings to the fore. There is no reason not to explain the Bible according to its literal meaning: Moses indeed took a Cushite woman as a wife. A Cushite, literally, is a person of black skin, and the prophet asked: "Can the Cushite change his skin?" (Josephus, in his *Antiquities*, quotes a story to the effect that Moses was king of Cush for forty years, and it was there that he took the Cushite woman as a wife. As far as we are concerned, this does not either add or detract from the story.) When Moses took a Cushite wife, Miriam and Aaron immediately claimed that he was no longer worthy of being the leader, and that they were more worthy than he — a claim whose echo has been heard among racists to this day, and which God rejected angrily.

Besides the prohibition of mixed marriages, there are a few cases in the Torah of discrimination between the Jew and the non-Jew. At the same time that "one shall not exact payment from his neighbor and his brother" during the sabbatical year, he may "exact payment from the stranger." By the same token, "You may take interest from the stranger, but you may not take interest from your brother." If the Jews wish to anoint a king over them, "you may not place over you a stranger who is not your brother." What the Jew is forbidden to eat he may sell to the "stranger." These laws, and others such as these, indicate that where the stranger is not specifically mentioned, the same law applies to the Jew as to the non-Jew. Thus Solomon opened the gates of the Temple "to the stranger who is not of Your people Israel." A non-Jew who observes the seven Noahide laws (the prohibitions against idolatry, blasphemy, incestuous relationships, murder, theft and the eating of the limb of an animal which is still alive, as well as the positive commandment to establish courts of law) "is considered to be of the righteous of the nations of the world." And R. Meir said: "Even one who worships idols and studies the Torah is like the high priest."

The law is that wherever the Torah specifies "your brother" or "your neighbor," it does not include the foreigner. Thus, for example, in regard to the return of a lost object, as it states, "every lost item of your brother," the Sages deduced that a lost object of a non-Jew need not be returned. Or in goring by an ox: as it states, "the ox of his neighbor," they deduced that a non-Jew need not be compensated for his damages. It is told of Rabban Gamaliel, that the Roman emperor sent two legal advisors to examine "the Torah of Israel and its nature"; he showed and explained everything to them, and when they left they said, "Your entire Torah is fine and praiseworthy except for one thing that you say, namely that the ox of an Israelite that gores the ox of a Canaanite is exempt (from paying damages), and the ox of a Canaanite that gores the ox of an Israelite must pay full damages." According to one source, they also added, "We will not inform the emperor of this thing." Again, according to one source, Rabban Gamaliel immediately decreed that there was not to be any discrimination between Jew and non-Jew in all these matters, and this "in order to avoid a desecration of (God's) name." We cannot know if Rabban Gamaliel abolished the discrimination between Jew and non-Jew because he had been convinced that this in itself was a "desecration of God's name," or because he was afraid that it would be a "desecration of God's name" if Rome found out. If the two legal experts had indeed promised not to reveal this discrimination to the emperor, then it would appear that the discrimination itself was something that not only the non-Jews found distasteful, but Rabban Gamaliel too.

The vision of the Jewish prophets was that in the End of Days there will be no difference between Jews and non-Jews. "This is the purpose that is purposed upon the whole earth: and this is the hand that is stretched out upon all the nations." All the nations will be blessed and praised "in truth, in justice and in righteousness." All nations will stream to "the mountain of the Lord's house which will be established at the top of the mountains, and will be exalted above the hills," and "My house will be called a house of prayer for all peoples." The prophetic ideal is not isolation, but the gathering of all nations from the four corners of the world under the flag of a single nation. No nation is unworthy of joining the kingdom of God "over all the earth."

V.

Idolaters and the Members of Other Religions

The main difference in the Bible between the Jew and the non-Jew is idolatry. At the same time that the non-Jew in the Bible is an idolater, the Jew is commanded not to have "other gods" together with the single God. "I am the Lord your God" — that is the first and most fundamental of the Ten Commandments. Whoever is an idolater, or who worships "other gods" cannot be a Jew; and not only is he not a Jew, but by his nature he is anti-Jewish. When we conquer Canaan, we are commanded, first and foremost, to remove from it every vestige of idolatry, all the asherah trees, all the temples, and not to leave a single stone on another in those places where the ceremonies of idolatry had been held.

The danger that the Israelite nation of the time would not become accustomed speedily to the one God and would not be weaned easily from the idolatries made of wood and stone, which one could see and hold, was an immediate and real danger. It is a fact that throughout the time we lived in Eretz Israel, at least until the destruction of the First Temple, there were always those who worshipped Baal, and not only the common folk, but the kings and ministers of the realm. Alongside the priests of God there were priests of Baal, and alongside the true prophets there were false prophets.

But Judaism knew no compromises: the monotheistic Jewish religion, the belief in a single God, was what made Israel into a

42

nation. The danger of assimilation among the idolaters, of returning to idolatrous ways, was and remained so constant and immediate a concern, that not only was it forbidden to take their daughters as wives, as we have already mentioned, lest they raise their children to idolatry, but Talmudic law even forbade negotiating with them, trading with them and being in social contact with them. Any benefit from them or their houses or their temples was forbidden. A woman was not permitted to remain alone in the company of an idolater, lest she be raped there and then, and it was forbidden for a man to remain alone with an idolater lest he be killed. Children were forbidden to spend time with idolaters, lest they be harmed in one way or another. It was forbidden to sell arms, knives or other weapons to idolaters, because the presumption was that they were murderers and brigands. One was also forbidden to sell cattle to them, for fear that these would not be used for food, but for sacrifices to their idols.

The law in the Torah, "You shall not bring any loathsome thing into your house," was explained as a prohibition against bringing into one's house anything that smacked in the slightest of idolatry. The wine and vinegar, milk, bread, oil and cheese of idolaters were forbidden to be eaten by Jews or for any other use from which Jews might derive benefit, either because they had been used in idolatrous ceremonies or because the Sages feared that these products were injurious to one's health, for one never knew what the idolaters might have put into them.

In Eretz Israel, it was forbidden to sell houses to idolaters. One was permitted to rent them houses, but not as residences and only for commercial purposes. It is obvious that one was forbidden to enter their temples and, heaven forbid, to derive any enjoyment from their religious ceremonies which might appear pleasing to the eye, just as there are rabbis today who forbid Jews to enter churches, or temples of other religions, and to derive enjoyment from the beauty of the architectural art or the statues or other decorations. But in a famous mishnah we are told of Pericles son of Philosophus, of whom we know nothing else, who once met Rabban Gamaliel in Acre, "in the bath house of Aphrodite." It appears that the Romans had built a bath house in Acre and had decorated it with statues, including a statue of the Roman goddess Aphrodite, for whom the bath house was named. Pericles said to Rabban Gamaliel: "It states in your Torah, 'Nothing of the cursed thing shall cleave to your hand.' Why then do you bathe in the bath house of Aphrodite?" Rabban Gamaliel told him: "One does not answer questions in the bath house" (i.e., one does not discuss questions of Jewish law in the bath house). Pericles thus had to be patient, until Rabban Gamaliel finished to bathe and left the premises, and then he heard from him: "I did not come into its realm, but it came into my realm," namely that the bath house had been there before the statue had been brought in: I need the bath house; what do I care that they put a statue there? "One does not say," Rabban Gamaliel goes on, "that the bath house is a beautiful decoration to Aphrodite, but rather that Aphrodite is a beautiful decoration to the bath house." The bath house is not like a temple made for the gods. It was not built to worship Aphrodite, but the statue was carved in order to decorate the bath house. And indeed we also find other monuments in many places, both of gods and of kings. In the synagogue in Nehardea, there was a monument to a king, and there was nothing wrong or bad with looking at it, provided that one did not do so for idolatrous purposes but in order to enjoy the beauty of the work of art.

The loss or destruction of monuments was considered to foretell evil, i.e., some blow or tragedy. We read that when R' Tanhum bar Hiyye died, all the monuments were destroyed. As to those in charge of these monuments, who cleaned, washed and guarded them, we are told that they were considered among the greatest people in the kingdom. So too are we told that when R' Johanan died, "the statues bent down," and it was said that there were no statues such as these.

The Christians and the Muslims are not considered and have never been considered to be idolaters. The laws that apply to idolaters do not apply to them. It is true that their rituals are different, their religions are different, but they too believe in one God who is invisible. One of the medieval scholars saw how the Greek Orthodox churches were filled with statues, and as a result ruled that the Greek Orthodox Christians were like idolaters, but his opinion remained a lone one. It was not accepted, because all the pictures of Jesus, for example, as well as the statues in their churches, were placed there to beautify the churches or to remind one of history, and they did not worship or pray to these pictures but to the invisible God whose place is in the heavens or in the upper spheres.

Yet true idolaters, even at the time of the Talmud, enjoyed certain human rights, even if this was beyond the measure of the law. "One asks how they are out of courtesy," one supports their poor as well as Jewish poor, one visits their sick as well as the Jewish sick, one buries and eulogizes their dead and comforts their mourners, and all "out of courtesy." Regarding the question of saving an idolater who is being pursued, there were differing opinions. The Mishnah states that "If someone is pursuing an animal or a person who transgresses the Sabbath or an idolater, one does not (attempt to) save the lives [of the pursued]." On the other hand, it is reported in the name of R. Eleazar b. Zadok that "an idolater's life, too, is saved." And preference is shown to non-Jews who are idolaters over Jews who are "heretics" or idolaters. R. Tarfon states, "If a person is running after him to kill a person or a snake is running to bite him, he may enter the house of an idolater but not the houses of [Jewish heretics], for [the latter] know the truth and deny it, while the [former] do not know and deny it."

The laws of murder are the primary arena for improper discrimination. It states: "He who sheds the blood of man, by man shall his blood be shed." This Biblical law, which, as we mentioned earlier, is the first criminal law, was given to the sons of Noah, long before the giving of the Torah. It is obvious that it applies to all sons of Noah, i.e., to the descendants of Shem, Ham and Japhet. "He who sheds the blood of man" implies every man.

But we have already said that when the Torah speaks of "your brother" or "your neighbor," these are interpreted to refer only to Israelites. Thus, for example, we are told, "If a man comes presumptuously upon his *neighbor*, to slay him with guile, you shall take him from My altar, that he may die." So too does it state, "But

45

if any man hates his *neighbor*, and lies in wait for him, and rises up against him, and smites him mortally that he dies." The word "his neighbor" excludes one who is not his neighbor, namely the idolater or non-Jew. If one who is not "his neighbor" is killed through guile, the murderer is evidently not subject to the death penalty. One who lies in wait for someone who is not his neighbor and rises up against him is evidently not considered to be a deliberate murderer.

A certain Isi b. Akiva asked a tremendous question: "Before the Torah was given, we were forbidden to shed blood" in general. "After the giving of the Torah, rather than the law becoming more stringent, did it become more lenient?" It was difficult for him, and for us, to understand how before the Torah was given the laws of murder were far more comprehensive than after the giving of the Torah, whereas the opposite would have been more logical: that after the giving of the Torah the law should have been more comprehensive rather than less so. Yet Jewish law states that if a person kills a non-Jew, the court does not kill him. Instead, his punishment is left to Heaven; and at least ethically and religiously, if not judicially, the murder of a non-Jew is as despicable as the murder of a Jew.

The Talmud does not offer an answer to the question of Isi b. Akiva. It appears that the answer to the problem that he raised should have been exactly the opposite, as we stated, and especially as there are other places in the Torah where the word "his neighbor" does not limit murder to one's "neighbor" alone. It states, for example: "You shall not murder," and it does not say: "You shall not murder your neighbor," or "You shall not murder your brother." And it states clearly: "He that kills *any man* shall surely be put to death." One could have referred to these general provisions and based the law on them.

Maimonides was evidently not at ease with the fact that a person who kills a non-Jew is not punished, as compared to one who kills a Jew. He therefore ruled:

> All those murderers who are not liable to be put to death by the court, should a king of Israel wish to kill them as a prerogative of the monarchy and to ensure order in the realm,

46

he has permission to do so. So too may the courts kill him as an *ad hoc* ruling; if the times demand it, the court has the permission to do as it sees fit. And if the king did not kill [these people], and there was no need for an *ad hoc* ruling to enforce matters, the court must at least subject them (i.e., the murderers) to many lashes close to death, and imprison them in extreme straits for many years, and torment them with all types of torments in order to frighten and threaten the other wicked people, so that this should not be as an obstacle (i.e., an inducement for others to follow these people's lead); they will then say: "I will refuse to kill my enemy as did so-and-so, so that I will remain free."

In our times and in our area, where it is not the Jewish court of law but a secular court that deals with criminal cases, any discrimination between one who kills a Jew and one who kills a non-Jew is inherently defective. Even if murderers are sentenced to life imprisonment today, they are not placed in "extreme straits," they are not beaten, nor are they given "many lashes close to death." But even if the modern-day criminal courts had employed the (original) Torah law rather than secular law, they would have had to punish equally one who killed or maimed a non Jew and one who killed or maimed a Jew. He has maimed a person — and that is all that counts.

One of the seven Noahide laws that all of mankind must observe is the prohibition against shedding blood. Non-Jews are not commanded not to shed the blood of Jews, but not to shed the blood of any person. And if that is the law for non-Jews, then for Jews, who were given the Torah and whose commandments exceed those of non-Jews a hundred-fold, it is certainly the law.

Now, every non-Jew who observes the seven Noahide laws, as listed in the previous chapter, not purely by chance but with the deliberate intention of observing them as such, is guaranteed his reward in the World to Come. These laws contain nothing about the Sabbath or about studying the Torah. We find expressions in the Talmud that a non-Jew who keeps the Sabbath or studies the Torah "is deserving of death." Non-Jews are forbidden to observe the

Sabbath, as they were told after the flood: "They shall not rest day and night." And they are forbidden to study the Torah, as it states: "Torah did Moses bequeath to us, an inheritance of the community of Jacob" — it is our inheritance, and whoever is not of us and studies it, is like a thief. Maimonides copied these sayings and ruled that they are the law. Even if we accept the interpretations of these verses, even though Jewish law does not explain them in their simple literal sense, there is nevertheless no basis there for a death penalty. The law should have been ruled in accordance with the saying by R' Jeremiah, who learned from the verse: "My statutes and My judgments, which if *a man* do, he shall live in them," that "even a non-Jew who observes the Torah is like the high priest."

VI.

The Stranger

The Hebrew word for a stranger, *ger*, is derived from the verb root *gur* — to dwell — and means a person who has come to dwell in our midst, even though in reality he is not a member of our nation. It refers to a person who was born to another people, in another land, and came to us of his own free will to live among us. In ancient times, strangers might come to live in other countries because of the famine in their own lands or because of persecution (then, too, there was political harassment by kings and rulers against those whom they did not like), or for other reasons — and this might include, for instance, slaves who had fled from their masters. It was not in vain that the Torah specifically prohibited returning a slave who had fled to his master, and we will yet discuss this in another context.

These strangers came without anything, and the word *ger* thus became a synonym for a poor person. Had the strangers been left to their own devices, they would have starved to death. Therefore the Torah repeats numerous times our obligation to accept strangers into our homes and to give them food to eat and clothes to wear (as proof of this obligation, we are told that God Himself, among His other attributes, "loves the stranger, to give him bread and clothing").

But it is not enough merely to give him food and clothing; he has to be treated as if he is part of the family. The Sabbath, for example, is not only the day of rest for yourself, your wife, and your children, but also for "the stranger who is in your gates." On the day that you yourself do not work, you are forbidden to insist that he should work; the Sabbath was given to the stranger, the non-Jewish foreigner, no less than it was given to you.

There were times when we ourselves were *gerim* (plural of *ger*). In regard to Abraham, we are told: "There was a famine in the land, and Abram went down to Egypt to dwell (*la-gur* in Hebrew) there, because the famine was severe in the land." So too in the Book of Ruth: "It came to pass in the days when the judges ruled, that there was a famine in the land. And a certain man of Bethlehem Judah went to dwell (*la-gur*) in the country of Moab." Just as Abram was a "stranger" in Egypt, so was Elimelech, the father-in-law of Ruth, a "stranger" in the land of Moab. And one can add many such examples.

The fact that strangers were exploited and forced to engage in heavy manual labor is seen clearly in the Book of Chronicles. There we read: "David commanded to gather together the strangers that were in the Land of Israel; and he set masons to hew wrought stones to build the house of God." The same was true with Solomon:

> Solomon numbered all the strangers that were in the Land of Israel, after the numbering which David his father had numbered them; and there were found a hundred and fifty thousand and three thousand and six hundred. And he set seventy thousand of them to be bearers of burdens, and eighty thousand to be hewers in the mountain, and three thousand and six hundred overseers to set the people to work.

These "overseers" were evidently work foremen. Thus we see that there were a large number of strangers, and they were of vital importance: it was they who did the heavy manual labor, and it would appear that already then the Israelites themselves avoided such work.

The prophet Ezekiel also instituted civil rights for strangers. When he spoke, in the Diaspora, of the division of Eretz Israel among the different tribes once the redemption came, he stated: When you draw lots about the division of the land, in order to determine who gets what, you are to divide the land "among you and among the strangers among you who gave birth to children in your midst; and they shall be to you citizens as the Children of Israel; they shall participate with you in the inheritance among the tribes of Israel." Logically, the strangers would remain such and would continue to live in our midst without the right of an inheritance; the prophet therefore came and made "the giving of birth to children" in our midst a naturalization process. When lots are cast for the land in Eretz Israel among the people who return to it, those strangers who were naturalized will also be entitled to their own tracts of land. And note that the test for naturalization here is not a religious one; even if they are idolaters but gave birth to children in our midst, they have this right.

It was the fate of our forefathers to be strangers in the Land of Egypt. The children of Jacob, who went down to Egypt, "were fruitful and multiplied and grew exceedingly mighty, and the earth became filled with them." They were evidently not an insignificant minority in Egypt but a minority of strangers. They were not of the country, and were not citizens of Egypt. All signs indicate that they did not accept, nor were they permitted to accept, the Egyptian religion, the Egyptian customs and the Egyptian life style, but they lived in something like closed and separate ghettos. In Egypt, too, as in Eretz Israel, the rulers used strangers, i e , us, as slaves; but they embittered their lives "with hard work, with mortar and bricks, and with all types of work in the field"; they did not regard us as people but tormented us, oppressed us, persecuted us, and killed our sons. Therefore, Moses' action, that he took us out of Egypt to Eretz Israel was considered to be a "redemption" — a redemption from the bitter fate of those "strangers" who were not protected by any consul, and whom the permanent residents of the land exploited cruelly with hard labor.

As we had gone through this bitter experience, this trauma of being "strangers" in a strange land, who were exploited terribly throughout, we were commanded in the Torah, not once but twenty-four times, to love the strangers living in our midst, not to exploit them and not to force them to engage in heavy manual labor, and to permit them to enjoy those benefits granted us. "You shall love the stranger, for you were strangers in the Land of Egypt."

Alternately, do not do to others what they did to you: what is hateful to you, do not do to others. It was not in vain that Hillel the Elder said, when a non-Jew came and wanted to convert, that in reality this was the entire Torah of Israel, and that everything else was but commentary.

And if at the time this referred primarily to the stranger who came from the outside, the stranger who found or who sought refuge among us from persecution, hunger, or any other type of distress, how much more must this be true with the people who were already living here when we came here. In this regard, there is no difference that we came here with a "divine" right; as valid and decisive as our right may be, we may not discriminate between one who came to us from the outside, and one who remained among us to find refuge.

It is true that we were commanded to destroy the "Seven Nations" that lived in the land, but, as mentioned, they have already been destroyed and did not leave over a living soul. But the law of loving the stranger applied even then to those who had settled among us, those non-Jews who came up with us from Egypt to Eretz Israel, that Egyptian "mixed multitude" and rabble, who thought that although they were unable to make a living in their own land, they could make a living with us. These and the members of all other peoples who are not part of the "Seven Nations" we must love, if they join us and live in our midst.

From where, then, do we find the negative conduct toward strangers? The prophet Isaiah said: "For the Lord will have mercy on Jacob, and will yet choose Israel, and set them in their own land: and the strangers will be joined with them, and they will cleave (in Hebrew, *ve-nis'pehu*) to the house of Jacob." The prophet used the word "cleave," a word which later served one of the sages of the Talmud as an excuse to say: "Strangers are as painful for Israel as a skin lesion" (in Hebrew *sapahat*). The two words really have nothing in common, but this analogy was later to result in the tremendous difficulties that are placed today in the way of those who come to convert, and we will yet discuss this.

In the Book of Job, the stranger is mentioned in the verse, "a stranger shall not lodge outside," the simple meaning of which is that if a stranger does not have a roof over his head, you are to give him one and to accept him into your home, and are to ensure that he does not lodge outside. A late Midrash used this verse to explain the verse in Isaiah in a much more comprehensive manner: that God does not reject any creature, but accepts all; the gates are open all the time, and whoever wishes to enter may do so.

> It therefore says, "a stranger shall not lodge outside" ... for in the future the strangers will be priests who serve in the Temple, as it states, "the strangers will be joined with them, and they will cleave to the house of Jacob."

But the strangers who will in the future "be priests who serve in the Temple" are not "the strangers" in the Biblical sense; the rabbis never considered for a moment that a stranger who was not a Jew could indeed serve in the Temple. Therefore the Talmud differentiated between the "righteous stranger" (*ger tzedek*) and the "resident stranger" (*ger toshav*). A righteous stranger is one who wishes to convert in order to accept the Jewish religion and to be a Jew in every way, whereas a resident stranger is a non-Jew who is unwilling to become a Jew, but, on the other hand, is not an idolater and has accepted the seven Noahide laws — "And why is he called a resident? because we may settle him among us in Eretz Israel" (Maimonides).

There is no such thing as "conversion" in the Bible; according to the Biblical law, every stranger is "converted" automatically; by the very fact that he is a stranger, he is a "convert." The process of conversion was only devised at the time of the Talmud, and only for "righteous strangers"; in other words, conversion was meant only for those strangers who wished to stop being strangers and wanted to become Jews; they no longer wanted to be strangers and foreigners, but wanted to become what we today would call naturalized, so that they would be accepted as if they had been naturally-born Jews. And indeed there is conversion for naturalization purposes — not for legal purposes but only for religious purposes — and it is different from the "naturalization" of the prophet Ezekiel, not only in the fact that as far as the prophet was concerned the stranger remained a member of his own religion, but also in the fact that as far as the prophet was concerned, the stranger enjoyed tangible material benefits, whereas the benefits that accrue from conversion are purely religious and spiritual. When a person has been converted in accordance with Jewish law, there is no difference between him and any Jew; from then on he is considered to be as if he is one of the descendants of the patriarch Abraham, and in most cases he is given the name Abraham son of Abraham.

In modern-day parlance, the *ger* is one who converted, and he is no longer a *ger* — a stranger in the Biblical sense. He is referred to as a *ger*, even though he has in reality ceased being a "stranger." But those strangers and foreigners who reside among us and live with us today, are no longer referred to by us as *gerim* — "strangers" — and not even as "resident strangers." They are treated as strangers and foreigners who have no status and no qualification within the Jewish religion. This is a deviation not only from the spirit of the Torah but also from its actual language. This is as the Sages stated: "The Torah will change in the future."

The Talmud states the law of conversion as follows:

> A stranger who comes to convert in these times, they say to him, "What did you see that you came to convert? Do you not know that Israel in these times are wretched and oppressed and enslaved and troubled, and suffer torments?" If he says, "I know and I am not worthy," they accept him immediately.

Rashi explains "I am not worthy" to mean "I am not worthy of participating in their troubles, and would that I will become worthy of it." Maimonides adds that at the outset one must investigate the person to see if there is any reason not to accept him — when the request for conversion was not made for its own sake but for another reason, or was not bona fide. The Talmud lists a number of "minor commandments and major commandments," as well as "the punishment and reward of the commandments," about which the judges must inform the prospective convert. Maimonides adds: "One informs him of the basic principles of the religion, which are the unity of God and the prohibition against idolatry, and one goes on about this at length," whereas about other matters, "one does not go on at length and does not demand the other commandments of him." After he has understood and accepted this, he is circumcised, and once the circumcision has healed he is immersed in a ritual bath. "Once he has immersed himself and come out, he is like a Jew in every way." Maimonides explains that the reason "one does not go on at length and does not demand the other commandments of him" is "lest one impose too much on him and divert him from the good path to an evil path, for at the outset one does not attract a person except through soft words of good will."

One who comes from outside the country and claims that he was a non-Jew and

> was converted by a Jewish court of law, is believed, for the same mouth that prohibited is the one that permitted (i.e., as the person could have avoided any question about his Jewishness by simply claiming he was born a Jew, we accept his word that he was born a non-Jew but converted). When is this true? In Eretz Israel and in the time that everyone living there was presumed to be a Jew, but outside Eretz Israel he must bring proof and afterwards he may marry a Jewess (Maimonides).

Only in a place where the majority are Jews is the man's word accepted, because of the basic principle that "one follows along with the majority," and if the majority of people are Jewish, the presumption about every individual is that he, too, is Jewish. There is also a view that since most people who claim that they are Jewish are indeed so, whoever claims that he is a Jew is presumed to be such. If a person is believed when he testifies that he is a Jew, either by birth or through conversion, anyone else who claims that this person is not a Jew must bring proof to his allegation. The problem that arises, as is known, is if a person claims that he was converted by a non-Orthodox Jewish court of law. Here, according to the Orthodox rabbinate, the person is not claiming that he "was converted according to Jewish law" or "in a Jewish court of law" in the meaning of these terms according to Jewish law. Thus his declaration is an admission, as it were, that he has remained a non-Jew.

But even if all of these people are not accepted as righteous strangers, they should at least be accepted as resident strangers; all of them observe the seven Noahide laws and all wish to live in Israel. It would appear that all the laws in the Torah of loving the stranger should apply to them — and at the least as an *a fortiori* argument: if these laws apply to non-Jewish residents as we stated, they should certainly apply to residents who claim, rightfully or not, that they are Jews and that they wish to cleave to Judaism. There is no need for the Torah to warn us to love the righteous stranger, because this love is subsumed under "You shall love your neighbor as yourself." In fact, we are told that righteous strangers are more precious to God than the people that stood at Mount Sinai. Only in regard to the resident stranger do all the admonitions to love the stranger apply. Possibly to enforce this requirement — one which is very difficult to observe in the spirit and language in which it was given — the rabbis ruled that the laws of the resident stranger only apply at the time that the jubilee year provisions are in force. As the jubilee year provisions are no longer in force, there are no longer resident strangers. This interpretation has been questioned, for it can simply abolish all the numerous commandments of the Torah which come to protect the "strangers," just as we were strangers in Egypt. It has been answered, though, that the meaning of the statement that the laws of the resident stranger do not apply only means that when there is no Jubilee year Jewish courts of law will only convert a person who wishes to become a righteous stranger, whereas resident strangers need no conversion or any other formal recognition by the court.

Thus we see that the perception of the Torah about the special "rights" of the stranger, which are clearly human rights, stemming from the special relationship of God to the stranger living in our midst on the one hand, and from our own experience as having been strangers in Egypt on the other, remain in effect — and as much as the commandments of love and the prohibition against oppression and discrimination are difficult for us, we are commanded, today as then, to observe them with every stranger who lives in our midst.

There are verses that we ourselves, the Jews or the Israelis, are but "strangers and residents" as far as God is concerned: "For Mine is the earth, for strangers and residents are you with Me." And King David added: "For I am a stranger with You, a resident as all my forefathers." And if for no reason than that we ourselves are strangers of God, who is the Owner of the earth, we have an obligation to relate to our "strangers" as we wish and pray that God will relate to us ourselves. This teaches us that we are not better or more privileged than they: just as they are strangers, so are we strangers; and just as God loves His strangers, so are we commanded to love our strangers.

I am inclined to believe that there has not been another judicial system, either in ancient times or in our times, which can compare, insofar as the rights of the stranger and the foreigner are concerned, to our Biblical law. Not only are we commanded that "a single law and a single justice shall there be for you and for the stranger who dwells with you," and that all — both the citizen and the stranger — must be equal under the law, but the stranger has a status which is, as it were, unique, stemming from his special right to love, a right which applies only to him and to the oppressed and persecuted who, because of this, need more concern and protection.

Meanwhile we have been strangers not only in Egypt but also in all the countries of our dispersion. And not only were we strangers in them, but there has not been a country in which we lived in which we were not persecuted. In recent generations we have been tested in the most horrifying manner, in ways unparalleled in human history. It is just this bitter experience that imposes upon us a holy obligation not to do to others what others did to us, and not to persecute any non-Jews among us, any strangers living with us in our land, but to love and support and respect them.

VII.

Slavery

A slave is someone who belongs to another person; his capabilities are not his own, his time is not his own, his goods are not his own, and even his wife and children are not his own; and he can be sold just as land can. There was no civilization in ancient times that did not have the institution of slavery; and there was no religion (including Christianity), or ethical and philosophical system (including the Greek) that did not accept the institution of slavery as self-evident, as if this was natural. If the Biblical law is different from all the other ancient systems, it differs in that it grants the slave certain "human rights," and at the time of the Talmud the Sages even added to these rights, until they totally abolished slavery.

We can differentiate between five types of slaves:

(1) The Hebrew slave: a Jew can become a slave if he stole something and does not have the wherewithal to repay what he has stolen, or if he refuses to return what he had stolen, and then "he is sold for his theft." A debtor who has no other possessions left to sell may sell himself: "If your brother waxes poor and is sold to you." King Solomon spoke of the fact that "the debtor is the slave to his creditor." The court, though, cannot sell a debtor for debts owed. Only he can sell himself.

(2) The Canaanite slave: "Of those who reside with you, from them you shall buy, and from their families with them which they bore in your land, and they shall be for you as an inheritance.

58

And you shall bequeath them to your children after you as an inheritance; you shall work with them in perpetuity." The implication is that there are strangers who live with you that are not "slaves," and there are strangers or the children of strangers who are your "slaves" — provided that you bought them. "Canaanite" is a generic term for all foreigners.

(3) War captives: They took "all the booty and all the spoil, of men and beasts," and divided them "among those who went out to battle, and among all the congregation." In another place, the taking of captives for slaves is limited to those cities where the other side surrendered without a battle: "If it greets you in peace and opens up to you, then all the people in it will be to you as tribute and will serve you." When, in the war between Israel and Judea, Hebrew prisoners were taken, the prophet Oded ordered that they be freed and that "the people of Judea and Jerusalem" should not "be taken for male and female slaves."

(4) The female slave: a Jew can sell his minor daughter as a female slave, at first possibly for marriage with the purchaser or his son. If the purchaser or his son then takes a second wife, the law stipulates that "her food, her raiment, and her duty of marriage, shall he not diminish," for otherwise he loses the money that he paid for her and she goes out "free without money."

(5) The children of slaves: It is a positive commandment to circumcise not only your sons, but also "the one born in your house and the one purchased with your money"; and the commandment to observe the Sabbath applies not only to you "and your son and your daughter and your manservant and your maidservant," but also to "the son of your maidservant and the stranger." If his master gave a Hebrew slave a female Canaanite slave as a wife and "she bore him sons and daughters," the latter remain slaves even if the slave himself is freed: the law of the "one born in your house" is the same as that of the Canaanite slave.

The major difference between the Hebrew slave and the Canaanite slave is that the Hebrew slave has a fixed period of slavery. In the case of a Hebrew slave sold by the court, he "shall work for six years, and in the seventh he shall go free." A Hebrew slave who sells himself can do so for as many years as he wishes — but only up to the jubilee year. The Canaanite slave, on the other hand, is a slave in perpetuity. The short period of slavery for the Hebrew slave sold to pay for his theft is based on the assumption that the debt for which he was sold, regardless of its size, will certainly be paid off by six years of servitude: "It shall not be difficult in your eyes when you send him free from you, for double the work of a hired man did he work for you for six years" — had you to pay a hired man, it would have cost you double. And not only can the period of involuntary servitude not exceed six years (excluding the case where the slave himself wants to remain beyond that time, "when the slave says to you, 'I will not leave you,' because he love you and your house, for it is good to him with you") — but a Hebrew slave only works until the jubilee year. In the jubilee year, "You are to proclaim freedom throughout the land to all its inhabitants." If the jubilee year comes and the slave has only worked three years or two years or even one year, he immediately goes free. Even a Hebrew slave who sells himself cannot do so beyond the jubilee year.

In the language of the Mishnah, a Hebrew slave "acquires himself with years, with the jubilee year, and with subtraction of money." By acquiring himself, he is released from his owner's possession and becomes independent in every way. The references to "years" and "jubilee year" are to the six years (or the period for which a person sold himself) and the jubilee which we mentioned above, which bring about his release, while "the subtraction of money" is the paying off by the slave of the balance of his debt; if the slave sold himself or was sold for five years for a debt of a hundred dollars, for example, and worked for a year as a slave, he can gain his freedom at that point by paying his owner the eighty dollars that he has not yet worked off (and the amount he has to pay is commensurately less if he was sold only a few years before the jubilee, so that each year of work represents a greater percentage of the debt paid). Whether his owner gave him pocket money which he saved up, or one of his relatives or friends gave him the money, the owner cannot refuse to free his slave when he is offered the "subtraction of money." If a Hebrew slave was sold to a non-Jew because of his debt, it is a positive commandment for "one of his brothers to redeem him," the reason being that the laws of the Torah regarding the treatment of slaves do not apply to Non-Jewish owners of slaves, and we are afraid that he will be treated the way slaves of other nations are treated.

One of the major differences between the laws of the other nations and the laws of the Torah is that among the other nations, as the slave is the owner's possession, he may do whatever he wishes with him, and even beat or torture him. This is not the case with us, where if a person hits his Canaanite male or female slave and harms either "his eye" or "his tooth," the slave must be freed. Just as this is true for the slave's tooth, it is all the more true for any damage to any essential organ. And even though a Canaanite slave generally has no standing in the court and cannot press charges independently because he is not master of his own body, once his owner injures him, the slave can press charges on his own and demand his freedom.

Owners can, of course, free their slaves at any time, by giving them a "bill of release"; but if an owner left his slave his goods as a bequest, that is regarded as a bill of release. The slave is also freed if his master dies, at least if the owner did not leave a son. The female Hebrew slave goes free when her owner dies, even if he left a son. Not only that: she is freed as soon as she shows signs of the onset of puberty. From this we see that a man may only sell his daughter if she is a minor, and immediately after the onset of puberty she is freed.

Slaves are considered to be "members of the household," and as such they inherit from their owners if the latter die without legal heirs. Abraham said to God about his slave Eliezer, "You have not given me seed, and the member of my household will inherit me." And we have already seen that a slave can be bequeathed his owner's possessions where there is no legal heir: "A wise slave ... will have inheritance with the brethren." Even though a slave who inherits his master goes free, there were evidently slaves who did not; thus we find that Ziba, the slave of King Saul, had "fifteen sons and twenty slaves," and David gave him the property of Mephiboshet, Saul's grandson. In the Talmudic period too, there were slaves who owned their own property; thus one accepts *shekalim* from slaves too, should they wish to contribute to the Temple maintenance. It is permissible to grant possession of an item to a slave "with the proviso that his master have no control over it"; and a pledge that a slave gave against a loan is returned to him after payment of the loan. But legally such possessions are the slave's only in order to increase his value, and with his added value, his sale price goes up. In the final analysis, though, the possessions that were bought by a slave enrich his master: "What the slave acquires, his master acquires."

In religious terms, we are all slaves, as it states, "For to Me the Children of Israel are slaves, they are My slaves that I took out of the Land of Egypt" — and whatever we have belongs to Him. Thus the prophet stated: "Behold, for your iniquities have you sold yourselves ... To which of My creditors did I sell you?"

And again: the fact that we ourselves are slaves to God, and that we were once "slaves" in Egypt, is what leads us to the conclusion that we are commanded to relate to the slave, who is like our total possession, as a person, as we would like people to relate to us. The Torah commanded: "For it is good for him with you" — and the Sages specified: "With you in food, with you in drink, with you in clean clothing; that you are not to eat white bread while he eats dark bread, you drink old wine while he drinks new wine, you sleep on down and he sleeps on straw." And what happens if a person has only one down bed? "If the person himself lies on it, he is not fulfilling 'for it is good for him with you,' and if he does not lie on it nor does he give it to the slave, that is the attribute of the Sodomites; thus the rule is that one must give it to the slave." "From this they (i.e., the Sages) said, 'Whoever acquires a slave for himself, acquires a master for himself.'" The Sages interpreted "For it is good for him *with you*" in a most literal way: it may be good for him, and he may be used to a simple, austere life, but you are not allowed to deprive him of the standard of living that you are enjoying; and if you cannot afford to support both of you, his needs come before yours, and his convenience comes before yours.

The Torah commanded: "You shall not rule over him (the Hebrew slave) with rigor" — and the Sages interpreted "work with rigor" to mean "work without a discernible end or work for which the person has no need" (make-work). What is work without a discernible end? It is work which was given in an unreasonable quantity, such as where the master said to his slave, "Hoe under the vines until I return," rather than saying to him, "Hoe under the vines as much as is necessary." And work which is unnecessary is where the owner assigns a task which is totally superfluous, such as telling a slave to hoe where there is no need whatsoever for hoeing.

So too did the Torah command, "Do not have him — and again this is a reference to the Hebrew slave — work the work of a slave; as a hired hand, as a resident he shall be with you." From this the Sages learned that one cannot force Hebrew slaves to do the work normally reserved for Canaanite slaves, such as "to carry his clothes behind him to the bath house, or to remove his shoes from his feet ... but he is permitted to cut his hair and to wash his clothes and to bake his dough, but he may not make him a bath house attendant for the public or a barber for the public or a baker for the public — and if that was his occupation before he was sold as a slave, then he may continue with it" (Maimonides). On the other hand, a Jew who is not a slave may be hired to take care of any of these duties — as a free man, he has the right to accept or refuse any given work. It is only the Hebrew slave, who must generally do whatever ordered to by his master, who is exempted from menial work.

One gets the impression that not only does a person who acquires a slave acquire a master for himself, but that there is no difference between the Hebrew slave and the hired hand. Only in regard to the way the owner has to treat the slave is there a difference: the owner must treat him like a hired hand, but he has to act like a slave. "How is that? You treat him in a brotherly fashion, and he acts to you as a slave." Or, in the words of Maimonides, "the slave must act as a slave in those works he performs for him" (i.e., the owner). In the last few words added by Maimonides, "in those works he performs for him," there is a significant limitation: whatever work the slave is assigned, provided that it is fitting work, he has to carry out without debate, but outside of work he is a member of your household. And there are those who explain "as a hired hand shall he be with you" as a commandment to pay him wages, as one pays a hired hand: "Just as a hired hand must be paid his wages within the day" (i.e., one may not leave the wages of a person who works daily from sunrise to sunset unpaid until the following morning), "here too must his wage be paid within the day." The meaning of this may possibly be that one must keep an accurate accounting of how much each day's work has decreased the balance outstanding on the slave. As to the verse that "for double the work of a hired man did he work for you," this is explained as the duty of the slave — for the slave and hired hand presumably do the same work during the same hours of the day — to work during the day and at night" — i.e., whereas the hours of a hired hand are fixed and definite, the hours of the slave are at the discretion of his owner. R' Isaac, though, has a different view: the double work of the slave as opposed to the hired hand is a result of the fact that his owner may give him a female Canaanite slave as a wife, and he now enjoys the work of the two as a couple. Not only that, but the slave can be forced to marry a female Canaanite slave "so that he will have slaves born from her, and she is permitted to him (as a wife) for the entire time of his work" (the language of Maimonides). In reality, the Canaanites were members of the "Seven Nations" that one is forbidden to marry; but what is forbidden for the owner is evidently permitted for the slave. When the slave is freed, though, if he came alone he leaves alone, and the woman and the children she bore to the slave are a net profit to the owner.

As far as human rights are concerned, the most important and revolutionary law in the Torah about slavery is the prohibition of returning a Canaanite slave to his owner if the slave had run away. (In the case of the Hebrew slave, he is to be returned, because he in essence has a work contract of a number of years that he must fulfill.) Thus the Torah states,

64

You shall not deliver unto his master the slave who has escaped from his master unto you. He shall dwell with you, in your midst, in that place which he shall choose in one of your gates, where he likes best; you shall not oppress him.

However, the limitation that was deduced by the Sages from the words "he shall dwell with you, in your midst," namely that this law only applies to slaves who fled from outside Eretz Israel to Eretz Israel, is not logical and is not in keeping with the simple meaning of the text. The Torah implies that this law applies to every Canaanite slave: whether he was oppressed or overworked or not; in all cases he is entitled to refuge, and every Jew must give him refuge.

This law has no parallel among the laws of any other nation, and even modern-day rights of sanctuary do not approach it. We have said that the Canaanite slave is the possession of his owner; when he flees, he causes his owner a monetary loss, and logic would indicate that the owner's "lost possession," his slave, should be returned to him. In other ancient law codes, the harboring of a slave who had run away from his master was considered to be a serious felony, even more serious than theft or armed robbery, for not only did the person harboring him make illegal gains, but by inciting the slave not to return to his owner or even merely harboring him, the person was considered to be an accomplice in depriving the owner of his possession. Not only does the Torah forbid a person to exploit a runaway slave or to enrich himself by him — and we will yet see how the slave gains his freedom by the very act of his fleeing — but it imposes on that person the obligation to protect the slave and not to oppress him. Furthermore, the person who gives him refuge must see to it that "it is good with him," even without benefiting from the slave's services. And not only that: the person must stand up firmly to the owner who pursues him or who demands his return — even if both are owners of slaves and have common property interests. In the conflict between property interests and respect for mankind, the Torah law prefers the person, his life, his respect and his security above any other value — even if the person is but a gentile slave.

The fact that the Torah gives the right of sanctuary to the

Canaanite slave (and to a person who killed another through negligence, as we saw before), proves that slaves running away from their owners were a quite common occurrence. Indeed, the slave had numerous and special legal rights — most of them significant, as that he was not to be beaten or worked with rigor, etc. — but there was no way open to him to assert these rights. He was at the mercy of his owner; should the owner wish to, he could violate these rights and torture his slave. From the Torah, it appears that the slave has the "right" to flee; it may well be that the exodus from Egypt can serve as a precedent for this. It is logical that a slave will not run away from a home where "it is good for him" and he is considered to be like a family member. When he flees, it is an indication that he is no longer able to live under the conditions of slavery that exist there. When the owner violates his obligations to the slave, the slave is permitted to run away, and no person is permitted to return him to his owner against his will. There is no better or more impressive sanction than that: the slave, even though he is your possession, is like a pledge in your hands — and you are liable to lose the pledge if you violate the law. There are those who say that the laws of the slave in this regard are meant to serve as a general lesson: just as with a slave, the right of refuge should apply to every other person who is persecuted. Thus did the prophet preach that one should hide those who are rejected and doomed to wander: "Let my outcasts dwell with you, Moab; be you a hiding place to them from the face of the spoiler."

The Sages of the Talmud — who were evidently more alert to capitalistic rights — felt that the denial of the rights of ownership that a master had over his servant was unjust. Even if the masters gave their slaves a reason for fleeing, the sanction of the loss of their property was not considered by the Sages to be in reasonable proportion to the owners' deviations from their authority (humane or legal). As mentioned, they at first limited the application of the Torah law only to slaves who had fled "from outside Eretz Israel" into it — as if there was no need for sanctions against Jewish owners in Eretz Israel that mistreated their slaves. But they did not want to deprive those living outside Eretz Israel of their legal possession.

Once a certain man whose slave had run away to Eretz Israel came to R' Ami, demanding that the slave be returned to him. In accordance with the decision rendered there, it was ruled that if a slave flees, his owner has to write a bill of release, whereas the slave has to indemnify his previous owner by paying him his — the slave's — value, as assessed by the court, from his future earnings as a free man. If the owner refuses to give him a bill of release the court has the right to "cancel the lien on him, and he goes free" (in the language of Maimonides). The same is evidently true if the owner is "outside Eretz Israel" or for some other reason does not present himself to the court. The solution found by the Sages for the injustice of freeing a slave without compensation was that the slave himself is to pay the compensation, the value to be assessed based on his value at the time that he fled. One may assume that every slave that despaired enough to flee was prepared to pay compensation from his future income, as long as he would be free and would not be returned to his previous owner. This was guaranteed him, for the Torah specifically stated that "You shall not deliver unto his master the servant who has escaped." Thus it is the fleeing by the slave that frees him from slavery, even when his owner is not willing to free him and receive compensation. By harassing his slave he has lost his possession, and by his refusal to free him he has lost his compensation.

We have no idea how many slaves who ran away from their owners indeed found sanctuary in accordance with the Torah law. The fact that the question was evidently raised for the first time in the court of R' Ami (at the beginning of the 4th century C.E.) is not an auspicious sign. Had the law been that a fleeing slave who sought refuge was required to work for the person who gave him refuge — and who was forbidden to send the slave away from his home — then the possibility of deriving benefit from the slave might motivate the person not to send the slave away empty-handed. But that is not the law: one is required to help him only in order to help him, to support him only to support him, to accept him into one's home only in order to save him from his pursuer — and for this one needs a tremendous and extremely rare amount of generosity — and especially when this law applies to a Canaanite slave.

If we can draw conclusions from the lack of generosity that our fathers showed in regard to freeing even their Hebrew slaves, it would appear that the observance of the commandment to help fleeing slaves and the prohibition against exploiting them would appear to be only an ideal and not reality. Zedekiah, king of Judea, had to make "a covenant with all the people in Jerusalem that every man should let his Hebrew manservant, and every man his Hebrew maidservant, go free"; and evidently "all the princes and all the people who had entered into the covenant" fulfilled their obligations. But a short while later, when they saw it was difficult to do without Hebrew slaves, "they changed, and forced the slaves whom they had let go free to return, and brought them into servitude as slaves." With this background, one can understand the fury of the prophet Jeremiah:

> You have not hearkened unto me, in proclaiming liberty, every one to his brother, and every man to his neighbor. "Behold, I proclaim a liberty for you," says the Lord, "to the sword, to the pestilence, and to the famine; and I will make you to be removed into all the kingdoms of the earth."

At the same time, I fear that these fiery speeches and the fulfillment of the prophet's words did not help. In the time of Ezra and Nehemiah, "there was a great cry of the people and of their wives against their brethren the Jews," because

> they bring into bondage our sons and our daughters to be servants, and some of our daughters have already been brought into bondage; neither is it in our power to redeem them; for other men have our lands and vineyards.

Nehemiah then said to the creditors,

> It is not good that you do ... Restore, I pray you, to them, even this day, their lands, their vineyards, their oliveyards, and their houses, also the hundredth part of the money, and of the corn, the wine, and the oil, that you exact of them;

and he managed to bring them to agree and to take oaths "that they should do according to this promise." What we see from the text is that the creditors not only seized their debtors' fields, vineyards and houses, but also "brought into bondage" their sons and daughters as slaves. All the prophecies and oaths and promises, all the commandments of the Torah, were not sufficient to restrain the evil lust for becoming wealthier and to prevent exploitation and oppression: the Sages of the Talmud thus saw a need to abolish the entire institution of slavery.

They were resourceful enough to do this not only without contravening the commandments of the Torah, but in a way that was made to fulfill them. We have already seen that in the jubilee year they had to "proclaim liberty" for all Hebrew slaves and to free them, even if the six year time period had not yet been completed; but once the jubilee year ceased to be observed from the Babylonian exile on, there was no longer the possibility of observing the commandment to free slaves with the onset of the jubilee year. Thus the entire institution of slavery was abolished. There are differences of opinion as to when the jubilee year ceased to be observed, but there is no doubt that at the time of the Talmud, after the destruction of the Temple, it was no longer observed. "Slavery" in the rubric of the Bible no longer existed.

Indeed, the Sages were not interested in totally abolishing the institution of slavery: slavery was prevalent throughout the ancient world and was considered to be something which was self-evident. Nor did the Sages presume to legislate for all of mankind. We are told that some of the Sages had slaves: Rabban Gamaliel mourned for his slave Tabi and "received those who came to comfort him," even though one does not observe mourning for Canaanite slaves; Rabban Gamaliel also said to his students: "My slave Tabi was not like the rest of the slaves; he was worthy." And the story is told of the "freed slave" of Tuvia the Physician, who testified with him regarding the sighting of the new moon. In this latter instance, there was a dispute as to whether the testimony of slaves was valid or not; the question could only arise in the case of a Canaanite slave, for a Hebrew slave was considered fit to testify. And we are told of cases where Jews even sold themselves and their children to non-Jews due to their financial distress.

The jubilee was only deferred during the period of exile, and it may be reinstated. Will slavery also be reinstituted together with it? Legally, slavery was not abolished but was deferred; and if anyone ever thinks of reinstating it at any future time in accordance with what is written in the Torah, he will do well to read what Maimonides wrote about this:

> It is a merciful quality and a wise course for a person to be merciful and to seek justice and not to impose too heavy a yoke on his slave or to torment him ... It states, "As the eyes of slaves to the hand of their masters and as the eyes of the female slave to the hand of her mistress" (and that is how our eyes turn to God). So too should [the owner] not humiliate [the slave] by deed or word — for slavery did the Biblical verse sell him, and not for humiliation. He should not scream at him too much or be excessively angry with him, but should speak to him calmly and listen to his claims. So too are we told of Job's correct ways, for which he was praised, (and Job stated): "If I did despise the cause of my manservant or of my maidservant, when they contended with me ... Did not He that made me in the womb make him? and did not One fashion us in the womb?" Cruelty and arrogance are only to be found among non-Jews who are idolaters, but the seed of our father Abraham, namely Israel, upon whom God bequeathed the good of the Torah and who commanded them righteous statutes and judgments, are merciful to all.

If this true with slavery, how much more without slavery.

We thus see that even from the laws of slaves one can find a humanistic and humanitarian Torah. In all the ancient nations, slavery symbolized inequality and the oppression, exploitation and rejection of those unfortunates who had no rights. Among us, even in the laws of slavery, with all the unacceptable discrimination in its very nature, we did not ignore the basic rights of man in that he is man. The cries of anger of the prophets and the preaching of Nehemiah and of the Sages prove how close to their hearts were these basic rights. The fact that they were violated arrogantly does not detract from either the observance or the value of these laws.

VIII.

Labor

The punishment imposed on Adam for having violated God's decree in the Garden of Eden was "with the sweat of your brow shall you eat bread," as if the sweat of one's brow from physical work is considered to be evil and a curse. In reality, God placed Adam in the Garden of Eden in order "to work it and guard it." The work and guarding that God imposed on Adam in the Garden of Eden was not only an obligation, but possibly, as we are speaking of the Garden of Eden, also a great privilege.

And indeed, work in general, and physical labor in particular, has remained both an obligation and a privilege in Jewish tradition. It is an ancient tradition, which found its expression in many sayings in the Talmud to the effect that a person is not allowed to refrain from working. Even if he wishes to devote the best of his energy and time to studying the Torah, which is one of the greatest and most important commandments, he is obligated to devote some of his time to work as well; to the extent that the Sages recognized but a few select individuals — as exceptions — whose learning was considered to be so important that they were permitted to devote all their time solely to the study of Torah.

In the Book of Psalms, for example, there are many words of praise for the man who works: "Man goes forth unto his work and to his labor until the evening"; "For you shall eat the labor of your hands: happy shall you be, and it shall be well with you"; and others. King Solomon advised: "He that tills his land will be satisfied with bread"; and:

Go to the ant, you sluggard; consider its ways, and be wise; which having no guide, overseer, or ruler, provides its food in the summer, and gathers its food in the harvest. How long will you sleep, O sluggard? When will you arise out of your sleep?

And in Ecclesiastes it states, "The sleep of a laboring man is sweet."

Even the lofty prophecy of the days of the Messiah is not one which states that all will sit and rejoice, but that the swords will be beaten into "plow shares" and the spears into "pruning hooks," i.e., into work tools, and the pleasure will lie in working the fields, with physical labor, for there is nothing to compare with it in returning to the days of the Garden of Eden.

This, indeed, is how the early sages taught. Shemaiah says: "Love labor and hate leadership, and do not draw close to the authorities"; i.e., do not think that if you sit and fill important positions as a community leader, you will gain happiness. On the contrary: love work and derive satisfaction and pleasure from that work.

Rabban Gamaliel, the son of R' Judah the Prince, said: "The study of Torah coupled with the way of the world (i.e., earning a livelihood) is admirable, for the labor in both drives away sin, and all Torah which does not have labor with it will eventually be nullified and draws sin in its wake."

R' Meir advised: "A person should always teach his son a clean and easy trade"; from this they deduced that a person should not teach his son a number of specific occupations, including that of a camel driver, a barber, a shepherd, and a storekeeper among others, these evidently not filling the bill of being clean and easy; or, as stated there, "their occupation is that of brigands" — as if it was to be presumed (in those days) that a storekeeper did not always earn his money by the most legal of ways. Thus it was better not to engage in trade and to engage in physical work.

But R' Nehorai says:

I will forsake all occupations in the world and will only teach my son Torah, for a person eats of its reward in this world, and the principal remains for the next world. The other occupations are not so: when a person becomes ill or old or in pain, and is unable to work in his occupation, he will die of hunger.

R' Nehorai also looked at this from a pragmatic point of view: he believed that one who devotes his entire life to the study of Torah will be preserved by God from all evil. But this is not the case with merchants and storekeepers and craftsmen, who, if they think they can survive without the help of God, will starve to death.

And we have the words of Ecclesiastes, "He has made every thing beautiful in its time," which the Sages interpreted to mean: "Every craftsman regards his own skill as the most admirable and effective"; "and God did this so that no occupation should be missing in the world" (*Rashi*).

On the other hand, we read, anyone whose occupation deals with women will have a bad end or will turn bad. There are those who explain this to mean that anyone whose practices are bad or whose associations are bad will not gain esteem from his occupation. But among the "bad" occupations that involve work with women, one finds ones that are esteemed in the modern era, including that of a goldsmith, perfumer, hairdresser, launderer, bath house attendant, and tanner. These occupations are considered to be despised and "turn one bad," evidently because they require ongoing contacts with women. Then, as now, various occupations and trades were ranked in accordance with the respect they enjoyed among the majority of the people — but such a ranking had no legal significance, except, possibly, in regard to anointing a craftsman as king. If you wish to choose yourself a king, first see what his occupation is, because one does not choose as a king "a butcher or a barber or a bath house attendant or a tanner" — not because they are ineligible, but "because their occupations are despised and the people denigrate them" (in the language of Maimonides), and the king has to be head and shoulders above the people, so that they will respect him and not disparage him.

And indeed, craftsmen and manual laborers enjoyed great respect. Even though there is a commandment in the Torah, "You shall rise before the hoary head," from which the rabbis deduced that one must rise before sages, they specifically exempted craftsmen engaged in their occupations from having to do so. Furthermore, they said: "Greater is the one who profits from his labor than one who fears Heaven," for in regard to labor it states: "You will be blessed and it will be good with you," whereas in regard to the fear of Heaven it states, "Blessed is the man who fears the Lord," but without the additional words, "and it will be good with you." This teaches us that one who lives off the labor of his hands will find it good for him not only in this world, but in the World to Come as well. As *Rashi* explains this saying of the Sages, "One who does not have enough to eat (i.e., because he does not have training in an occupation) will go to the crossroads and rob people," thereby endangering his life both in this world and the World to Come.

The Sages always knew that idleness can bring a person to sin — and a father has not fulfilled his obligation to his son if he has only taught him Torah without teaching him a trade (some say that a father must also teach his son to swim, "lest he be in a boat that sinks, and will endanger his life if he does not know how to swim").

R' Eleazar would say that just as the Jewish people were commanded to observe the entire Torah and especially the Sabbath, so too were they commanded to labor, as it states: "Six days shall you labor and do all your work." In this verse, the commandment to labor comes before that of the Sabbath, and is, in essence, the background for the Sabbath rest. After all, if a person does not labor and do all his work during the six days of the week, he has no need for rest on the Sabbath. Just as you are commanded to rest on the Sabbath, so too are you commanded to work on the other days of the week.

"Great is work," says R' Judah the Prince, "for if one is not occupied with work, people talk about him: 'From what (financial source) does he eat? From what does he drink?'" In order to stop people from whispering that someone is living off immoral funds, it is better that he should have a good and honest occupation which is apparent to all.

"And God saw all that He had done, and behold, it was very good." On this verse, one of the sages remarks: "If this is true for God, how much more so for an artisan." He, the great Creator, who is omnipotent, rejoiced at what He did, and saw that "it was very good"; how much more will an artisan rejoice at the product of his work and of his hands.

"A person who has a craft, what does he resemble? a fenced vineyard which no domestic or wild animal can enter, and whose produce is not eaten by passersby or seen by passersby." He can arrange his entire life within the confines of that craft, to the best of his ability and desire, and he is not dependent upon others. Just as "a woman who has a husband, whether she adorns herself or does not adorn herself, is not looked at by everyone" because they are afraid of her husband, a man who has a craft is not talked about by others.

Furthermore, Maimonides praises work as being beneficial to one's bodily health:

> One principle did they state about bodily health: as long as a person exerts himself physically and strenuously and is not sated and his innards are not weak, no disease will befall him, and his strength will be fortified.

Work is an essential condition for a healthy body. And one is commanded to labor "not only to accumulate money, but in order to gain those things that the body needs."

Yet, in spite of all these commandments, a person can say, "I am free to decide what I will do with my time and what I will not do with my time." If he specifically desires to remain idle, he may do so. If he wishes to study the Torah, he is certainly permitted to do so, but the preferred advice is to work in an occupation, to engage in physical labor, and not only because one earns a living wage thereby.

We find that a person is only *obligated* to work in order to earn the means to support his wife and children. If he does not have sufficient funds to support his wife and children, he can be forced to hire himself out so as to earn money to support them. This obligation is one that the husband signs in his marriage contract — the *ketubah* — in which he states: "I will nourish and support and clothe you (i.e., his wife) and see to your needs." This obligation is regarded as an agreement which forces the husband to hire himself out and work even against his will.

Let us now move to the rights of workers. Ancient Jewish law is different from other legal systems in that the labor contract obligates the employer, but not the employee. If the employee, for example, obligated himself to work a full day, he can change his mind even in the middle of the day. If he obligated himself to work for a month, he can say after a week, "I have had enough, I do not want to go on." And why is this so? because it states: "For to Me are the Children of Israel servants," from which the Sages deduced: "They are My servants, and not servants of My servants." If that is the law with slaves, it is all the more true with employees. From this we learn that even if a person obligated himself to work for a given time, he can always change his mind. He does not receive pay for the time that he did not work, but only for the time that he did. If he received his pay in advance, he must return the relative portion based on the time he did not work.

At the end of the Middle Ages, in the 15th century, the rabbis ruled that a person does not have to give any reason why he has decided to discontinue working, and why he is not prepared to fulfill his obligation to complete the work he had contracted for. But there is one reason for discontinuing his work which is unacceptable, to the extent that one can force the person to fulfill his obligation, and that is if he indicates that he wants to discontinue his work because he feels that the wage that he had agreed upon is too low. In this instance, one forces him to continue; if he agreed to a certain wage, he has to be content with that wage. However, if he says, "I don't want to work anymore because my wife is ill," or because his child is ill and he wants to take care of the patient, he may stop working. What must be made clear here, though, is that even if there are conditions which are in the contract stipulating various provisions of the work, these are not considered to force the person to continue to work: the contract is only in regard to the wages to be paid, and the different conditions in it only apply as long as the contract is in force. There is a major principle in Jewish labor law, though, that everything is "in accordance with the custom of the place" — by this we mean the custom of the place on the one hand, and the custom of the particular occupation on the other. If it is the custom

76

in a given place or within a given occupation that people work seven hours a day, then that is the amount of time that workers have to work daily, and if the custom is that there is a specific wage for this work, they are entitled to demand it. Even if the custom differs from the implied agreement, the workers can insist that they be paid in accordance with the customary wage scale — at least as long as there has not been a specific agreement to the contrary. The custom also determines whether the employee is entitled, in addition to his wage, to other fringe benefits.

Not only can there be a contract between a particular worker or a particular group of workers and an employer, but the members of a certain occupation can make a general agreement which will be binding on all members of that occupation. In reality, the concept of collective agreements of our days already existed at the time of the Talmud. Thus, "the wool workers and the dyers, the bakers and the sailors, the bath house attendants and the barbers" (and these are undoubtedly merely examples) can agree among themselves about the way they will work and the conditions related to their work.

In the Bible, too, we find labor laws that have been influential throughout the generations, as, for example: "When you come into the vineyard of your fellow, you shall eat grapes as you desire to your contentment, but you shall not put (of them) into your utensils"; "If you come into the wheat field of your fellow, you shall harvest ears with your hand, but you shall not lift up a sickle"; and "You shall not muzzle an ox while it is threshing." The right is granted to the worker to eat as he desires at the employer's home or in his field or vineyard as long as he is working; but he is forbidden to take any of the food home. The employer is not permitted to demand that the worker take the "straw and hay" that he is producing in lieu of his wages — even though the value may be the same — but must pay his worker in cash.

We have already mentioned that one's day worker must be paid by the following morning, and if the employer does not do so, he violates a prohibition. The Torah repeats this prohibition a second time in an almost brutally explicit manner:

You shall not oppress a worker who is poor and needy, whether he is of your brethren or of your strangers that are in your land within your gates. On his day you shall give him his hire, neither shall the sun go down upon it, for he is poor, and sets his heart upon it; lest he cry against you unto the Lord, and it be a sin unto you.

There are differences of opinion among the sages of the Talmud as to what is considered "oppression" of a worker. According to one view, oppression is the putting off of the worker from day to day — "Do not tell your fellow, 'Go and come back, and tomorrow I will pay you,' while you have the wherewithal to pay." According to a second opinion, "oppression" here refers to a person who denies that he owes a worker money that the worker had indeed worked for. A third opinion is that the "oppression" referred to here is that of an employer claiming that he had never ordered the work to be done in the first place. If, however, the employer refuses to pay the worker for his labor, without denying his obligation and without other excuses, it is not considered to be "oppression" but "theft." It is a law of the Mishnah that "a day worker collects (his wage) the entire night (i.e., he must be paid before the night ends), and a night worker collects the entire day, while an hourly worker collects the entire night and the entire day." In the case of a weekly or monthly or yearly worker, should the period for which the worker was engaged conclude during the day, he collects the entire day; whereas if he concludes working at night, he collects the entire night and the entire day. Not being punctual in paying wages is like "taking the soul of" (i.e., "killing") the worker, who eagerly awaits his wage. If there is a dispute between the employer and the worker about an outstanding debt, the worker "swears and takes" — swears that he is owed the money involved, and is believed and paid accordingly. Why then does he need to swear in the first place? "In order to assuage the mind of the employer." When the worker comes to the court and demands his payment, "one does not act stringently with him ... but one acts leniently with him and begins by telling him, 'Do not vex yourself — swear and take'" (in the words of Maimonides).

We have already mentioned that workers have the responsibility to be punctual and to be careful in their work. While they deserve, *ex post facto*, to receive support "beyond the measure of the law," at the outset they have the responsibility to be diligent and careful. "All artisans are paid watchmen" — the raw material that was handed to them for processing is considered as a pledge for which they are responsible, and the employer is entitled to set off against their wages the damages that the artisans cause him. Already in the Middle Ages, though, the rabbis had ruled that the employer cannot claim more in the court than a declaration of his rights: *ex post facto*, based on the precedent in the Talmud, the employers must give their workers their due, even if the workers may have caused damages to their employers' materials.

There were occupations that were considered to be so difficult or so community-oriented or so respected that their wages were paid by the Temple treasury, i.e., the public purse, including in this category "the checkers of blemishes" in humans and animals (the equivalent of today's doctors or veterinarians), "Torah scholars who teach the laws of ritual slaughter to priests," "women who. weave the ark cover," as well as "the checkers of the Torah scrolls in Jerusalem." *Rashi* explains that the latter refers to the checkers of scrolls owned by individuals,

> because one is forbidden to keep in one's possession a scroll that has not been checked, due to the prohibition of "do not allow corruption to reside in your tents." As the court saw that the people (who had ordered the scrolls) were opposed to paying (for this check), they placed the Temple treasury in charge of this.

Among those who received their pay from the Temple treasury were "the judges that judge the brigands in Jerusalem" — but I am not sure why this only applied to the judges of thieves and not to judges in general.

IX.

Women

The equality between men and women is expressed forcibly in the story of the creation of the world: "And God created the man in His image, in the likeness of God He created him, male and female He created them." And another verse repeats this verity: "This is the book of the generations of man — on the day that the Lord God created man, in the likeness of God He created him, male and female He created them, and He blessed them and called their name Adam." Even if we say that Adam was created first and Eve was built up from the rib that God took from Adam's body, the woman was nevertheless created in the image of God, and was created for the purpose of being equal to and a partner with man in everything: "And they were a single flesh."

All ancient legal systems involved inequality between the sexes, and the results of this inequality are evident in our society to this day. In theory, and as a matter of principle, the only exception to the rule is the Torah: "And these are the judgments that you are to place *before them*" — on this verse, the Sages expound: "The Torah equated women to men for all the laws of the Torah." And not only for the "laws," but also for the punishments: "If a man or woman is guilty of any of the sins of man" — "this equates women and men for all sins and damages in the Torah." If we look at these provisions, and at the fact that God created both male and female in the image of God, and that the same name was given to both — for God "called their name Adam" — one can see in the provisions a type of basic rule: unless stated differently in a specific law to that effect, the Torah equates men and women completely.

Before we turn to those areas where there is detrimental discrimination against women, we will first take a look at discrimination that is to their benefit, i.e., where women are exempted from obligations which are obligatory in the case of men. A father is required to fulfill numerous commandments in regard to his son — to circumcise him, to teach him Torah, to marry him off, to redeem him from captivity, etc. These commandments are obligatory for the father, but not for the mother. On the other hand, women are commanded to respect their parents, just as are men. Women are generally exempted from commandments that must be performed within a fixed time frame. This exemption has different interpretations and explanations. There are those who learn it from the verse which states: "Three times a year shall your males appear before the Lord your God in the place which He will choose, on the Festival of *Matzot*, on the Festival of *Shavu'ot*, and on the Festival of *Sukkot*" — this verse refers to the three pilgrimage festivals. There are those who deduce from this that just as this commandment is limited to "all your males," so too are all other time-related commandments limited to males. Others state that the source is not based on interpretations of the text, but on pragmatic grounds: all the time a woman has is devoted to her husband and her home, for the needs of her home impose on her various restrictive or select commandments: she is engaged in taking care of her home the whole day and a good part of the night (in accordance with the verses, "her light will not be extinguished at night"; "she rises also while it is yet night, and gives food to her household, and a portion to her maidens"), and one cannot ask that she drop everything to fulfill those commandments that must be performed at a given time. One should note that when we speak of "time-related commandments," we are only referring to positive commandments that must be carried out at a given time; but as far as negative commandments or prohibitions are concerned, these apply to women equally as to men. Thus a woman is not permitted to desecrate the Sabbath or to eat leaven on Passover — but she is

81

exempt from putting on *tefillin* every weekday morning.

If a woman wishes to, she is permitted to perform all or some of the time-related commandments, but there are those who hold that as women are not commanded to perform them, they cannot expect any reward for their performance. The aggadah relates that Michal, Saul's daughter, would put on *tefillin* each day — even though this is a time-related commandment, being operative during the day and not at night — "and the Sages did not protest this." If one wishes to claim that this aggadah is a painfully inadequate source upon which to base the right of a woman to observe all the commandments, including those singled out for men, one may rest assured that the rabbis of our times are violently opposed to those women who trespass into male preserves, be these the putting on of *tefillin* or serving in the rabbinate.

And there are commandments that women are exempt from for physiological reasons, such as "You shall not round the corners of your heads" (i.e., the prohibition against shaving the sideburns, for if one does, one's haircut appears to be as round as a bowl), and "You shall not destroy the corners of your beard" (the prohibition against shaving with a razor). Then again, there are certain commandments that can only apply to women, because of their physiology, such as that of immersing themselves in a ritual bath after their menstrual emission.

The first commandment in the Torah, "Be fruitful and multiply, and replenish the earth," even though stated in the plural form in Hebrew, does not apply to women — the commandment to "be fruitful and multiply" applies only to men:

> Men are commanded about being fruitful and multiplying and not women. R' Johanan ben Beroka says: "Regarding both of them (i.e., both men and women) it states, 'be fruitful and multiply.'"

Some interpret "be fruitful and multiply" not as a commandment but as a blessing, and then all agree that the blessing applies to both men and women. If, though, the verse is meant as a positive commandment, it only applies to males, for it states later in the same verse, "and replenish the earth *and conquer it*," which the rabbis interpret as applying to men, for "it is the manner of men to conquer, and not the manner of women to conquer." The fact that the male must be the active one and the initiator in such matters, is deduced from the taking of the rib from the body of the man in order to create the woman: "Who seeks after whom? the one who has lost something searches for that which he has lost." But that does not mean that women are exempt from punishment for illegal acts of sexual intercourse. Woman are specifically equated to men, as it states, "Both the adulterer and the adulteress shall surely be put to death." So too is it stated in regard to incest: "Both did an abomination, their blood is on them" — not because the woman is considered to be the one to have carried out the forbidden act, for she is regarded as having a passive role, but because the Torah considered "the enjoyment derived as equivalent to the act."

Even though women are not obliged to give birth to children, their desire to have a child, to "be fruitful and multiply," is so natural and so strong — and therefore so legitimate — that a husband who is sterile can be forced to give his wife a divorce.

And just as there are various commandments which do not apply to women because they are time-related, there are others from which women are exempt because they are not in keeping with respect for women as women. As we saw, a man can sell himself if he cannot pay his debts, or can be sold by the court if he is unable to repay a theft that he stole, but only "a man may be sold for his theft, while a woman may not be sold for her theft." There is also a difference in the way that capital punishment is administered: "A male is stoned while naked, but a woman is not stoned while naked; a male is hanged (after having been executed) but a woman is not hanged." When both a man and a woman need charity, the woman takes precedence; if a man and a woman were taken prisoner and there is only enough money to ransom one, the woman takes precedence. When a man's body and a woman's body need to be buried, the woman's body takes precedence. If a man and a woman are waiting in line, for example, to hear the verdict against them in court, the woman takes precedence. A girl cannot be "wayward," not only because the Torah speaks of a "wayward and rebellious son" (*ben sorer u-moreh*) — the penalty for which in theory is death — but because it is not normal for a girl to be a glutton and a drunkard. There are also those who explain that the reason why women are not valid as witnesses or judges is because "the entire glory of a woman is inward," within her home, and a woman should not be demeaned by having to become involved in the often sordid goings-on in the courtrooms.

As to the discrimination against women, all of it stemmed from the inferior status of women in the ancient, patriarchal society, with "each man the ruler in his home" — an absolute ruler. In reality, the Torah placed numerous restrictions on the rule of the husband, limiting the custom that had prevailed from ancient times; and the Sages of the Talmud added further limitations. At the base of everything, though, lies the principle that a man "takes" a wife, while a woman does not take a husband; a man divorces his wife, and a woman does not divorce her husband. While it is true that a woman may be "acquired," her husband does not "acquire" her, and the Sages ruled that a woman can only be married of her own free will; Rabbenu Gershom Meor Ha-Golah added a ban of excommunication upon whoever would divorce his wife without her knowledge and approval. There are grounds for the view that the "acquisition" is shunted aside by the "*kiddushin*," the marriage: while in ancient times men would "take" a wife as a possession, later, at the time of the Mishnah, they instituted *kiddushin*, in which the man "sanctifies" (*mekadesh* in Hebrew) his wife, and acquisition as such — even though it is yet mentioned in the ancient mishnah — disappeared from the world. A woman who "sanctifies" a man to herself has accomplished nothing, just as a woman who attempts to divorce her husband cannot accomplish anything. The Hebrew word for husband, *ba'al*, implies ownership and lordship, and it is he, as we mentioned, who is the active one and the initiator. In reality, though, the man has no "ownership" over his wife, and the prevalent use of the word *ba'al* in modern Hebrew today to connote a husband is an indicator that it has lost its original meaning. Not only can't a husband sell his wife as a slave to pay his debts or his theft — although he can sell himself — he cannot impose on her every type of work or service. If she does not fulfill her obligations as a wife, his only recourse is to sue her in court, although her actions may possibly be considered grounds for divorce.

At first, whenever a husband found anything distasteful about his wife, he was permitted, at his own discretion, to write her a bill of divorce and to give it to her. To prevent this situation of anarchy, the Sages decreed that every bill of divorce must go through a Jewish court and with its permission.

By the *kiddushin* (and the *ketubah* — the marriage document, which follows this), the husband promises to supply his wife with "her food, her raiment, and her duty of marriage" — i.e., to supply her food, clothing and sexual needs. All these are rights to which the wife is entitled, and obligations of the husband toward her; but if she refuses him sexual contact, she is liable to be considered to be "rebellious," and to be forced to accept a divorce. She has the right to "rebel," but she must accept upon herself the result of her rebellion, for she knew why "she entered the wedding canopy." As to her food, the law of the Talmud is that her husband is entitled to all "the products of her hands," including not only her time and her work, but also her wages from working outside. But he is permitted to set off her food with the money she earns. So too is he entitled to her income from her property. In addition to her food, and separate from it, the husband is responsible for her medical costs, for redeeming her from captivity, for burying her, and for her support from his estate after his death.

The discrimination which is the worst as far as the married woman is concerned is the institution of polygamy; the husband is permitted to marry additional wives whenever he wishes to, whereas she is limited to one husband as long as she is married to him — he is the "sanctifier," and she is the "sanctified one." Whomever a man "sanctified" to himself is his legal wife. The terrible sin of adultery only applies where a man lies with the wife of another, or if a married woman lies with a man who is not her husband; there is no adultery if a married man goes to bed with an unmarried woman. And even though Rabbenu Gershom imposed a ban on a person marrying more than one wife, thereby forbidding polygamy, its echoes and implications are felt to this day. If the court ruled that a certain woman must be divorced from her husband, and the woman refuses to accept the bill of divorce, the court can grant the husband "permission to marry," which permits him to marry a second woman, even though the first marriage is still in effect; whereas if the husband was ordered to divorce his wife and refused to do so, the court cannot permit the woman to marry another man. (This is the origin of the many *agunot* — the "chained women" — whose husbands have refused them a divorce, and who cannot free themselves of the chains of their marriage.) The same discrimination occurs in cases of mental illness: if a woman is incapable of accepting a divorce because of her mental illness, her husband is permitted to marry another woman (after 100 rabbis have signed to permit this, this procedure being the counterweight to the ban of Rabbenu Gershom). If a husband, however, is unable to grant his wife a divorce because of mental disease, even a thousand rabbis do not have the power to permit the woman to marry another man. And we already find in the Mishnah: "A man who divorces does not resemble a woman who divorces, because the woman leaves (the state of matrimony) with or against her will, while the man only has (the woman) leave if he so desires" — and this differentiation exists to this day, in spite of all the bans of Rabbenu Gershom. (The reason given by Maimonides for permitting divorce because of mental illness, "that sane people are unable to live in the same home as simpletons," only applies, surprisingly, when a man must live in the same house as a mentally ill woman, but not when a sane woman must live in the same house as a mentally ill man.)

Another case of blatant discrimination is that a husband inherits his wife, but a woman does not inherit her husband — just as sons inherit their father, while daughters do not inherit him, but are supported by their dead parent's estate. "When there are substantial assets," the sons can enjoy their inheritance even when the daughters take their support from the estate, but "when the assets are meager, the daughters are supported and the sons go begging at the doors." As the sons inherit their father's assets, they have to pay the debts owed by his estate. In the Talmud, Admon asked: "Is it just because I am a male that I should lose?" Rabban Gamaliel felt that there was substance to his argument.

A person can "write his assets" to his wife, by writing a will in her favor; but so deeply rooted was the tradition of inheritance by the sons, that such a will was regarded as appointing of the widow as the guardian of the estate, and after her death the estate would return to the sons. If the husband specifies that his widow will not only handle his estate but will inherit it (or part of it), then indeed she becomes his heir, but the husband's estate is regarded as including within itself all the possessions of the wife which he is required to return to her in accordance with the *ketubah* — the marriage document.

The Sages commanded that a person must respect his wife more than himself, and must love her as himself. If he has money, he must support her in accordance with his wealth. He should not impose upon her excessive fear, and must talk to her calmly. He is not to be sad or hot-tempered (the language of Maimonides), because "blessings do not rest upon a man's home save because of his wife." A person is never permitted to distress his wife, for "her tears should not be frequent." It states in the Torah that the woman (Eve) was "the mother of all life" — to teach us that she only marries to have a good life, a life of wealth and not a life of poverty, a life of respect and not of being despised; "she goes up with him but does not descend with him." If he claims that in her father's house she was used to poverty and he can therefore keep her in those same conditions, his claim is dismissed.

Abraham was commanded: "Whatever Sarah says to her, listen to her voice"; and thus the Sages of the Talmud advised that a husband should always consult with his wife, at least on those matters dealing with "the house" and "the world," as opposed to heavenly matters.

(As we are dealing with the rights of the wife, I have deliberately left out her obligations to her husband.)

A woman may not be crowned as a sovereign, as it states, "From the midst of your brothers shall you appoint a king over you" — "your brother and not your sister." Alexander Jannaeus, however, commanded that after his death he should be succeeded by his wife, and thus we had the reign of Shlomzion (Salome Alexandra). Not only did the Sages not protest against her appointment, but they even praised her and her deeds, and in her days and at her initiative the Pharisees resumed their leadership role. The blessing of Heaven also rested upon the reign of this woman, "for we find that in the days of Simeon ben Shetah and in the days of Queen Shlomzion it rained on Friday nights (this is referred to in the Torah as "rain at its appointed time," for rain at this time does not disrupt the farmers in their work, the Sabbath being their day of rest), and the crops throughout this time were extremely bountiful.

In days of yore we had women prophets. Three of them are mentioned by name in the Bible, these being Miriam, Deborah and Noadiah, to which the Talmud adds four other names, for a total of seven women. The Bible also tells of "wise women" who were consulted; and in the Talmud there is extensive praise of Bruriah, the wife of R' Meir, who was famous among the Talmudic scholars. They even exaggerated and claimed that each day Bruriah would study 300 laws from 300 different great Torah sages, and this for a period of three years. To all these we must add Deborah the wife of Lapidot, who was both a prophet and one who "judged Israel" as the leader of the nation.

The fact that even in the ancient patriarchal society, and in spite of her inferior status, a woman could attain the heights of the spirit and of leadership, using her own talents, proves that there is not — and there never was — anything which could withstand the force of a talented woman.

The prohibition that "a woman may not wear that which pertains to a man" was explained as if to prohibit a woman from serving in the army or of bearing arms. It is possible that this interpretation was strengthened in the words of the prophet, "Behold, your people in the midst of you are women; the gates of your land shall be set wide open unto your enemies." And indeed women may be included, by their nature, in the category of those "who are fearful and fainthearted," whom the Torah exempts from military service, "lest his brethren's heart faint as well as his heart." But the law in the Mishnah states that in a "*mitzvah* war" — one which is defensive — "all go out, even a groom from his chamber and a bride from her bridal canopy."

X.

Prophets: Freedom of Speech

At first blush, it would appear that there is no freedom of thought or of speech in religious law. By its nature, religious law is based entirely on belief in God, in His mercy, in His justice, in His absolute rule, and there is no place for opposing or other opinions or for opposing or other speech. But the ancient Biblical law, which is the basis of Jewish tradition, is replete with examples of freedom of thought and speech, even with an obligation to say what one thinks in his heart.

In the Jewish legal system, as in other legal systems, one deduces "freedom of speech" from the limitations on speech. As slander is forbidden, as are other types of talk, it must mean that those areas that have not been prohibited are permitted: "From the negative one deduces the positive." There is in the Bible, for example, a grievous sin, and that is to incite people to idolatry. One who says, "Let us go and worship other gods," is considered to be a dangerous criminal. The inciter of those days was considered what we would call a traitor today; a traitor, too, can commit a crime simply by his speech. By inciting others with his speech, a person can be a traitor to God. And indeed, this prohibition is defined and limited: whatever is not outright incitement to idolatry is not included in the prohibition; and as "there is no punishment unless there is prior warning" that a specific action is forbidden and punishable, one does not punish those who incite people to other acts besides idolatry.

90

Prophets: Freedom of Speech

So too are there prohibitions such as "Do not bear tales among your people" (the prohibition against slander), or "Do not curse the deaf" (which was later expanded to cursing of any kind), or "You shall not curse the judge, and a leader in your nation you shall not curse" (which includes not only cursing God, but also cursing or insulting a king or a judge), "Do not swear in My name falsely," "Do not lie one to another," "Do not take the name of the Lord your God in vain," "He who expresses the name of the Lord will surely be put to death" (the prohibition against pronouncing God's actual name), and "If a man curses his father or his mother, he shall surely be put to death" — all these are clear prohibitions, which limit freedom of speech. Indeed, every legal system limits freedom of speech in order to protect other individuals, the state, its religion or other values.

Logic would dictate that in a religious legal system it would be enough merely to deny God, without actually cursing Him, in order to commit a prohibited action. The statement by Isaiah, "Shall the clay say to him that fashioned it: 'What are you doing? Your work has no handles?'" simply indicates how absurd the very denial of the existence of God is. But denial of God is not a felony that is punishable by death, unlike cursing God or using His ineffable name or inciting to idolatry, all of which are. Of course denial of God's existence is a sin, but it is only punishable by God, when and how He decides, but not by the courts, because this action was never listed as punishable.

Indeed, from the first days that the Israelites left Egypt, "the people complained": they had various complaints against God and against Moses, without any restraint. And they were not always punished for it, even when their protest constituted derision or revolt. Not only did they dance around the Golden Calf immediately after the giving of the Torah at Sinai, proclaiming, "These are your gods O Israel," but when they did not receive the fleshpots that they so craved, when they were not given everything they wanted (today we would refer to wages, but then they referred to food) they began doubting, "Is God in our midst or not?" For the 40 years that they travelled through the desert, God imposed severe punishments upon them: Korah and his flock were swallowed up in the ground; Miriam, who had spoken out against Moses about the Cushite woman he had taken, was punished and became "leprous as snow"; the spies who had given an evil report of Eretz Israel died in a plague; and the people who had lusted for meat died in their masses at *kivrot ha-ta'avah* — "the graves of the lust." And God, as it were, lost His patience more than once: "How long will this nation provoke Me, and how long will they not believe in Me?" And this was symptomatic not only of the generation of the desert; throughout Biblical times we find that the Jews did not refrain from rebellious comments; when they felt they had a legitimate complaint or were bothered by something, they expressed themselves about it.

Indeed, the most typical manifestation of freedom of speech in ancient Jewish history was neither negative nor positive — and here we refer to prophecy. Already in the Torah, God promised that He would raise up from among the Jewish people prophets such as Moses, and He would instruct them what to say to the people. So too did He command us to obey the prophet, and He reminded us that God was speaking through the prophet's mouth.

Indeed, there arose prophets among us whose prophecies manifested freedom of speech; and the fact that they spoke in the name of God is immaterial. The true prophets not only claimed to speak in His name, but believed with all their hearts that everything uttered by them was directly from God. As opposed to the true prophets, there were thousands and tens of thousands of false prophets, who also claimed to speak in God's name, but their inspiration was not necessarily divine. They used freedom of speech not in order to spread the word of God and God's ethics, but in order to curry favor with the kings and rulers of their days. These were in most cases the prophets with good tidings, while the true prophets were the prophets of outrage; what all had in common was freedom of speech. As far as the true prophets were concerned, this freedom became an obligation and was vital: "For Zion's sake I will not hold my peace, and for Jerusalem's sake I will not rest." There is a view that the prophets were poets, patriots, statesmen, critics and geniuses in the art of speaking and of style: public rhetoric was their daily bread, and their voices were heard on the heights from every platform, in the markets and the streets — whether the rulers or their audiences liked it or not. They were not intimidated to stop prophesying and were not afraid to rebuke, in the strongest terms, the rulers or the people for their sins; or the priests who did not fulfill their duties properly; or, especially, the false prophets who competed with them, who claimed to prophesy in the name of God without having been authorized to do so. As to freedom of speech, the prophets did not recognize any censorship and had no hesitation in attacking their opponents in the sharpest of language; and they did so in a triumphant style and with the greatest rhetorical flourishes.

I have mentioned that we were commanded to obey the prophets and everything that they said, and I have always regretted that the prophets almost never utilized their legislative authority and did not add statutes and judgments to their ethical preaching. They evidently were not yet aware of their authority, for the phrase, "to whom you shall hearken" was only interpreted at the time of the Talmudic Sages as meaning that whatever the prophets said was obligatory. In any event, they chose to leave their ethical preaching for posterity, and it is around this banner that we unite. It was not for naught that the phrase "the peace and justice of the Jewish prophets" was included in the Declaration of Independence of the State of Israel, and it is this banner which guides the Jewish state in its special path.

How can one differentiate between a true prophet and a false prophet? The Torah states, "If you say in your heart: 'How will we know if the thing was not said by the Lord?'" What is the identifying sign of the false prophet who claims to speak in God's name and was not authorized to do so? The Torah supplies us with a simple test: "If the prophet speaks in the name of the Lord and the thing does not occur and does not come, that is the thing that the Lord did not speak." Wait and see: if the prophet's prophecies are fulfilled, it is evidence that he is a true prophet, whereas if they are not, it proves that he is a false prophet. The Mishnah expands on this a little, and states: "One who prophesies in the name of idolatry," one who admits that the source of his inspiration is idolatry or who speaks in the name of other gods, is revealed as a false prophet *ipso facto*, and there is no need to wait to see if he prophesied truly or falsely, even if his prophecy "was correct as far as the law is concerned regarding whether an object should be ritually pure or ritually impure" — and all the more so if he claims to change the law. Only if he does not claim to speak in the name of idolatry, and it appears on the surface that he is a true prophet, is there no choice but to wait to see if his prophecy is fulfilled.

Here too Maimonides differentiates between the prophet who bears good tidings and the one who bears bad tidings. When a prophet bears good tidings, there is no choice; one has to wait to see whether his prophecy is fulfilled, for if it is fulfilled it is proof that he is a true prophet, and if it is not fulfilled he is a false prophet. But if the prophet brings bad tidings there is no need to wait, because if his prophecy is not fulfilled, and instead of the evil there is good, that is but a sign that God has been merciful. God loves to retract evil decrees, just as He retracted the decree against "Nineveh this great city," whose destruction Jonah had preached. But if the evil tidings are fulfilled, as was the case, for example, with the prophecy of Jeremiah, it is a sign that he is a true prophet.

Prophecy had actually begun during the era of Moses, of whom we are told: "There arose none in Israel" like him. God commanded him to gather together 70 of the elders of Israel, who would prophesy in the Tent of Assembly. There were two men, Eldad and Medad, who prophesied within the camp, outside the Tent of Assembly. Joshua, Moses' faithful servant, became enraged at them for violating the law and prophesying outside the Tent of Assembly, and beseeched Moses: *Kela'em.* The commentators differ as to the meaning of the word *kela'em.* If we explain it according to the simple meaning, it implies placing them in a *keleh*, a prison. If that is the case, this is the first recorded instance of an attempt to imprison people for using their freedom of speech improperly or in a place where they had no right to use it. Alternately, the meaning is that Joshua asked Moses to silence them. In either event, the

94

response by Moses was a remarkable one: "Would that all the people of the Lord were prophets, and that the Lord would impart His spirit upon them." I will not punish them or shut them up, and I will certainly not place them in prison: would that every single member of this nation was a prophet who could prophesy, in every place and at every time.

But some prophets were not able to evade the punishment of the kings against whom they had preached. Amos prophesied, for example, that Jeroboam would die by the sword and Israel would be exiled from its land. And Amaziah said to Amos, "O seer, go, run away to the Land of Judea and eat bread there and prophesy, and do not continue prophesying in Bet El, because it is the seat of the king and of the monarchy." Here your life is in danger: the king will pursue you and punish you. And we hear of a prophet named Uriah ben Shemaiahu of Kiryat Ye'arim, a man who "prophesied in the name of the Lord," "of this city and of this land, according to all the words of Jeremiah," namely that the people would be taken into captivity and would be killed by the king of Babylon. Jehoiakim the king heard of this, and wanted to kill the prophet, and Uriah understood the danger involved and fled to Egypt. One would imagine that by fleeing he would have saved his life, but the king sent men to Egypt, "and they took Uriah out of Egypt and brought him to King Jehoiakim and he smote him with a sword, and he cast his body to the graves of the members of the people." It was only by a miracle that Ahikam ben Shafan saved Jeremiah, "so as not to give him into the hands of the people to kill him."

But Jeremiah, too, suffered greatly; he was imprisoned twice in the "pit" and was put on trial by "the priests and the prophets," who told "the princes and all the people saying, 'This man deserves the death penalty, for he prophesied about this city as you heard with your ears.'" Jeremiah succeeded, by means of a brilliant speech in his own defense, to be declared innocent: "This man is not deserving of the death penalty, because he spoke to us in the name of the Lord our God." This teaches us that sometimes an excellent defense can prevent a conviction.

The important message that the prophets of Israel, led by

95

Jeremiah, gave us, is that a person who utilizes freedom of speech to propound unacceptable views or sharp criticism, or an angry protest, always assumes the risk of persecution, besmirchment and punishment, and can even endanger his life, until he agrees to shut his mouth. Freedom of speech is entrusted to those of a strong spirit and who are brave, and who will not forsake the battlefield. The prophet Jonah fled "before the Lord," so as not to have to prophesy destruction upon that large city. His fate shows that nothing was accomplished by his flight, and one who has been summoned to arise and protest is not permitted to forsake his mission. Indeed, his flight was atypical: the prophets always excelled in their steadfastness, without fear or apprehension. Nathan stood before King David, Elijah stood before King Ahab, and there were many others like them. And they did not only prophesy to their monarchs about the terrible blows that would descend upon them from heaven, but also made clear their views about the evil ways of the kings, who, rather than serving as models of rectitude to the people, had corrupted all the good values of ethics and justice.

The prophet did not only issue warnings about "those that decree unrighteous decrees ... to turn aside the needy from judgment, and to take away the right from the poor of My people," and about the oppression and the thefts which the rulers had perpetrated, but also called upon those who had been oppressed or robbed to rise up and protest the injustice: "He was oppressed, and afflicted, yet he did not open his mouth; he was brought as a lamb to the slaughter, and as a sheep is dumb before its shearers, so did he not open his mouth." There is freedom of speech, or there should be, for those who are oppressed (or especially for those who are oppressed), so that their cries can be heard. And the right to cry out carries alongside it the obligation of being heard: it is a divine attribute, for "if you oppress him, I will surely hear his cry."

At the same time that the Bible tells us of the existence of many hundreds of false prophets (the 850 prophets of Ba'al and the Asherah that were gathered together by Elijah, and the 400 that prophesied to Jehoshaphat king of Judea), the Talmudic tradition lists the number of true male prophets at 48 (and another 7 women prophets whom we mentioned earlier). Thus we see that the true prophets were always a minority — and indeed those who need freedom of speech are always the minority; the views that the majority wishes to propound are the views that the majority wishes to hear, and there is no one to protest against them.

"From the day that the Temple was destroyed, prophecy was taken from the prophets and was given to the Sages." If this statement refers to the First Temple, then it is clear that prophecy was not taken away from prophets such as Ezekiel, Haggai, Zechariah and Malachi; and if the reference is to the Second Temple, one is unable to see where the "prophecy" of the *Tanna'im* and *Amora'im* after the destruction exceeded that of the Men of the Great Assembly and the first *Tanna'im*. Be that as it may, the Sages of the Talmud found support for themselves in the Torah for their conclusion that "a sage is greater than a prophet": the prophet must first prove himself by having given "a sign or a wonder," while a sage does not earn his position based on signs and wonders but by his wisdom and learning.

But the destruction of the Second Temple did not mark the end of those among the Jewish people who have cried against injustice, or who have expressed the opinion of a minority or of a single individual; but none of them (or any other person) has claimed for himself the mantle of prophecy. Just as the prophets prophesied under divine inspiration, so too did the Sages teach their oral Torah as if it had been given Moses at Sinai: they may have needed to first announce that prophecy had ceased in the world, lest doubts arise whether a later "prophecy" might be preferable to Jewish law; or they may have proclaimed that prophecy had ceased in order to prevent people being drawn to the "prophets" of Christianity. In any event, ever since prophecy was given to the Sages, its voice has not been stilled — and its special values have received new dimensions and a different framework.

XI.

Sages: Freedom of Opinion

R' Eleazar ben Azariah expounded on a verse in the Book of Ecclesiastes:

"The words of the wise are as goads, and as nails fastened by the masters of assemblies, which are given from one shepherd." Who are the "masters of assemblies"? These are the Torah sages who sit in assemblies and study the Torah; these (sages) declare something ritually impure and those declare it ritually pure, these forbid and those permit, these invalidate and those approve. Should a person then say, "How shall I now learn Torah?" — How can I find my way in this convoluted thicket of differences of opinion, of different Torahs? — It therefore teaches us: All were given from one Shepherd, the one God gave them, one Guide said them, from the mouth of the Master of all Creation blessed be He, as it states: "And God spoke all these things." You too are to listen attentively and to acquire a heart that understands the words of those who render something ritually impure and the words of those who render it ritually pure, the words of those who forbid and the words of those who permit, the words of those who invalidate and the words of those who approve.

It appears that this saying of R' Eleazar ben Azariah expresses one of the remarkable concepts of the oral Torah. It is a most "pluralistic" Torah; there is almost no problem, be it legal, ethical or other, where there are not disputes. One says something is acceptable while another says it is unacceptable; one says no and the other says yes; one says it is permitted and the other says it is forbidden. Can one possibly determine a Jewish law that one must follow? Although it was possibly unavoidable that, over the course of time, different ways would be found to determine the law until it was finally laid down as authoritative, at the beginning there were marked differences of opinion, with freedom of speech. Each sage expressed his own tradition, his own opinion, his own interpretation, his own logic, and each one had reasons for his own decision. As they found students who followed in their paths and these students gained their own students, various schools were developed which competed with one another and argued with one another — the most famous of these being the School of Shammai, which was generally more stringent, and the School of Hillel, which was generally more lenient. In order for the law to be determined in accordance with the School of Hillel, where "these say the law is in accordance with themselves and those say the law is in accordance with themselves," and where both were sincerely convinced that their tradition was the true Torah — a divine voice had to emanate from heaven and to announce that "both these and those are the words of the living God, but the law is as the School of Hillel."

This was not the only time that a divine voice came forth from heaven to determine the law between conflicting views, between "words of the living God" that contradicted one another. Once, when R' Eliezer argued against the majority and tried to use all types of supernatural signs and wonders to prove that he was correct, he failed to impress his colleagues. Finally, he summoned the ultimate authority and said, "If the law is in accordance with me, let the heavens prove it." A voice came forth from the heavens and said: "What do you have against R' Eliezer, for the law is in accordance with him in every place." Logic would dictate that just as with the School of Hillel, here too they would regard the voice from heaven as decisive; but here R' Joshua, who was the spokesman for the majority, arose and said that the Torah "is not in the heavens," and we no longer "pay attention" to any voices from the heavens. Instead we make our own decisions, "for it was already written in

99

the Torah at Sinai that 'You are to follow the majority.'" In questions related to the Torah, which is no longer in the heavens but upon the earth, one follows the majority. This revolt, as it were, against the divine decision, and this stand for the freedom of human opinion and human decision-making, has no parallel in any other religious legal system; it appears that it made an impact in heaven as well, for the Talmud goes on there that at that time Elijah the prophet heard God say with a smile, "My sons have defeated me; My sons have defeated me." It is a pity that the events did not end with this remarkable story. After the majority won the battle, they misused their power and authority and revenged themselves on R' Eliezer by excommunicating him.

Following "the majority" is indeed an easy and logical way to determine the law when there are two conflicting opinions, but it cannot eliminate the differences between the two viewpoints. Even the minority view, which is not accepted as the law, represents "the words of the living God." Not only should a person who expressed "the words of the living God" not be excommunicated for his views, but for there to be a decision in accordance with "the majority," as opposed to a unanimous consensus, there must be a minority to dispute the majority. Thus we are told: "Had the Torah been given as a clear-cut document, there would have been no room for any learned man to render any decision in law." The Torah was not given "clear-cut" and unequivocal, so that each learned scholar would be granted the right to render decisions in accordance with the law as he understands it. A Torah which was "clear-cut" from the outset, as it became over the generations in that the law was determined and frozen, would not have left any room for discretion to the "words of the living God" as reflected in differing ways and conflicting views.

The verse, "God has spoken once; twice have I heard this; that power belongs to God," is understood to mean: "A single verse can be understood in a number of ways." And the words of the prophet, "as a hammer splits asunder a rock" were explained to mean: "Just as a hammer causes a number of sparks to fly, so too is a single verse interpreted in a number of ways." And elsewhere: "Just as a hammer causes a number of sparks to fly, each utterance from the mouth of God was split up into 70 languages." And no single explanation (or language) is more legitimate or less legitimate than any other; by the very nature of the living Torah it has various meanings, and there is room for varied interpretations.

It is said that in R' Meir's generation there was none like him: And why did they not determine the law in accordance with him? Because his colleagues were unable to fathom the depths of his thought, for he would say that something ritually impure was ritually pure and prove it, and that something ritually pure was ritually impure and prove it.

It appears that R' Meir's brilliant mind visualized the different conflicting views of all the sages. As R' Meir loved to bring up different views, it would seem that he was capable of showing reasons for both permitting and forbidding the same act, and for indicating what was true and what false in each view. The reason his colleagues were "unable to plumb the depths of his thought" was that from time to time he contradicted himself, and retracted a view that he had expressed earlier. *Rashi* explains that his colleagues were unable to understand "which of his views were correct and which were incorrect, for he would give a thought out and logical explanation for every single law" — in other words, he evidently was able to take a certain proposition which was not in accordance with the law and give a persuasive argument to prove that it was in accordance with the law, or should be in accordance with the law. And if indeed his reasons were persuasive, whether this was indeed the law or whether it was desirable that this should be the law, then not only was there no reason not to rule in accordance with him, but there was good reason to rule like him. Possibly the meaning of their not being "able to plumb the depths of his thought" is that they were unable to differentiate between the times that he spoke as a legislator, when as a judge and when as an academic; when he spoke *ad hoc*, and when he spoke for posterity.

"R' Meir had a student named Symmachos, who would give 48 reasons why an item which was ritually impure was so, and 48 reasons why an item which was ritually pure was so." This

101

statement indicates that not only was R' Meir able to teach his students to differentiate clearly between the ritually impure and the ritually pure, but also that he had the ability to pass on to his students his powers and his sharpness, which enabled him to find numerous reasons why something ritually impure should be so and why something ritually pure should be so. But neither R' Meir nor his students had the reputed ability of "a veteran student of Jabneh," who knew how "to declare a *sheretz*" — a dead rodent, which by Torah law is ritually impure — "pure for 150 reasons."

What we see from the above — and we are able to add numerous examples such as these — is that in those ancient study halls there was freedom of opinion and freedom of speech; and even though there was a limitation that a student had no right to render a legal ruling in the presence of his teacher, this principle was based on good manners and respect for the teacher. (In capital cases appearing before the Sanhedrin, the youngest colleagues were the first ones to express their opinions, so as not to be intimidated by their elders.) According to the Talmudic tradition, the Sages would "contend" with one another; not only would they debate and exchange views, but they would defend their views, even if they were in the minority.

We have learned: "Every dispute which is for the sake of Heaven will eventually endure ... Which is a dispute for the sake of Heaven? that is a dispute between Hillel and Shammai." The disputes between Hillel and Shammai are but an example of all the disputes in the Talmud; all were for the sake of Heaven, and that was why all of them endured throughout the generations. And as the views of both are "the words of the living God," there is no justification to accept one over the other. The fact that the law was determined in accordance with one of them and not in accordance with the other does not add to the divinity of the former nor does it detract from the divinity of the latter.

The question, "And why does [the Mishnah] mention the words of the individual alongside that of the majority" is one that already preoccupied the sages of the Mishnah, and there are differences of opinion about this as well. One sage (the "former *Tanna*") says that the reason for the inclusion of the views of an individual in the Mishnah is so that if a Jewish court of law wishes to rule in accordance with the individual even though the authoritative ruling was not in accordance with that individual, another court cannot "annul the words of its fellow court unless it is greater than the original one in wisdom and numbers." Of course the court could be prevented from relying on the view of an individual as against the majority, or one might decrease the danger of a court's relying on an individual, had the view of that individual not been mentioned and had only the view of the majority been brought down. Thus, by bringing down these views of individuals, the Sages sought to leave the option open for a specific court to prefer, for its own reasons, the view of the individual — and if it did so, the law would be valid until invalidated by another court greater than it "in wisdom and number." R' Judah says the reason the view of an individual is quoted, even though the law is not in accordance with him, is "that if a person says, 'I have a tradition to this effect,' they will say to him, 'You heard it in the name of so-and-so'" — and the commentators explain that they will say this to him so that he will know that what he has was but the view of an individual, and the law is not in accordance with him.

But this mishnah can be explained in a different way: if a person comes and testifies that he has a tradition from his father or his teacher to act in a certain way, he is told that he is not acting in accordance with the decided law but in accordance with an individual who differed with the majority, and may rest easy. This interpretation is corroborated by a version of the text attributed to the same R' Judah in the *Tosefta*; he argues there with the view that the reason given for the mentioning of the opinion of an individual is so as to reject that opinion. Instead of this, he gives as the reason for the retention of the opinion of an individual, "lest a time may come where they will rely on it." In other words, even if the law at present is in accordance with the majority, there may come a time when they may find it necessary to rule in accordance with the opinion of that individual. And this is indeed the most logical reason: if one mentions the opinion of an individual merely to discount it, it would be best not to mention it at all and to allow it to be forgotten over the years. (And that is what Maimonides does in his *Mishneh Torah* when he only mentions the view of those in accordance with whom he has ruled, so that "the oral Torah will be clear to all, without questions or answers, and not to have one person saying thus and another thus.") The preservation of all opinions, and not only those that are actually in effect in Jewish law, was meant for future generations — and not only so that the ruling should be different should changing times require it, but also to perpetuate the character of the oral law, which represents the sparks flying from a rock which has been struck by a hammer.

But freedom of opinion is not a monopoly of the Sages; the aggadists expressed the concept underlying the basis of general freedom of thought and found support for it in the Torah itself. When Moses prayed to God, he referred to Him as "the God of the spirits," rather than "the God of the spirit," and the aggadists expounded on that use of the plural. Moses beseeched God before his death "and said to Him, 'Lord of the Universe! You know the views of every person, that the views of one are not as the views of the other. When I leave them, I beg of You, if You seek to appoint a leader over them, appoint over them a person who will suffer each one in accordance with his views.'" The "leader" is the legislator and the ruler — who must be willing to "suffer" unacceptable views, even if the "suffering" is only an apparent one. The leader must suffer the differences among them, whereas the people must recite a blessing over these very differences: "If one sees a large number of people, one recites the blessing, 'Blessed is the Wise One of the Heights' — just as their faces are not identical, so too are their views not identical; rather each has his own view." That is the way the verse, "To make the weight for the winds" is explained — to give weight to each individual view. God, "the Wise One of the Heights," knows the secrets of everyone and his views, and it was not for naught that He gave each person his own views. It is for this reason that one recites a special blessing when seeing a multitude of people.

Legally, too, each person is allowed to hold his own opinions, even if these are improper or criminal. As long as his deeds are not forbidden ones, he does not commit a sin. "Things in the heart are irrelevant" — this was said in regard to civil law, but it applies to criminal law as well. Oral utterances, even if they are forbidden ones, are not considered to be criminal, but in the category of "a negative commandment which does not involve an action." And criminal charges cannot be brought for mere utterances (except for specific sins that involve speech, such as an oath in vain, the cursing of God or incitement to idolatry). Should one then wish to claim that such matters are not punishable by man but are indeed punishable by God, our Sages state: "An evil intent is not joined together by the Holy One, blessed be He, to an action."

This is not true, though, from the religious perspective: there are unacceptable views that, should a person "say" them, result in his "not having a place in the World to Come," as, for example, "if a person says that there is no revival of the dead in the Torah, and that the Torah is not divine." The same is true for the *apikorsim*, these being, in the language of Maimonides, those who say

> that there is no such thing as prophecy, and there is no feeling which comes from the Creator to man's heart, and one who denies the prophecy of our teacher Moses, and one who says that the Creator does not know the deeds of mankind,

and the *minim*, whom Maimonides classifies as those who say that "There is no God and the world does not have a leader, and a person who says there is a leader but there are two or more, and one who says there is one Master but that He has a body and a form ..."
In another place, Maimonides describes *apikorsim* as those who "follow the dictates of their hearts in stupidity, until they deliberately violate the basic precepts of the Torah without hesitation, and claim that there is no sin in doing so." Note, though, that those consigned to the fires of hell are not those who *think* these thoughts, but those who *say* them, or act in accordance with them.

There is one felony for which the penalty is death, which at first consisted of no more than expressing an opposing view. The Torah states, "If a man acts deliberately and does not listen to the priest ...

or to the judge, that man shall be put to death." From the context, it appears that this refers to a person who deliberately refuses to act in accordance with a ruling by an authorized court. However, the Sages interpreted this to refer to a *zaken mamreh* — a "rebellious elder" — namely one of the group of legislators or judges, who differs with his colleagues and maintains his own position: "This is how I expounded it, and this is the way my colleagues expounded it; this is how I taught it, and this is how my colleagues taught it." The sages of the Talmud evidently believed that a death penalty should not be imposed for not obeying a ruling of the court, and they thus sought for themselves a different context for this capital offense. But the expressing of an opposing view, and even the stubborn maintenance of that view, does not justify so stringent a penalty, or even any penalty — and they therefore limited the sin of the verse, "who *acts* deliberately" to an elder who was authorized to instruct others in the path to follow, and who instructed them "to act" in accordance with his view and not in accordance with the view of the majority: "If he instructed (people) to *do*, he is culpable ... and he is not culpable until he instructs (people) to *do*." And indeed, public order requires that the individual legislators should not all decide the law for themselves, for if there are various laws by different people and these conflict with one another, they cause chaos in the world, or, in the words of the Sages, "they increase disputes in Israel." The *zaken mamreh*, though, is given three opportunities, before three courts, to persuade the court that his ruling or his tradition or his logic is correct and that the majority view is incorrect, and if he is rebuffed three times and still continues ruling in accordance with his view, he commits a sin. He is permitted to continue to hold his view, and even to express his view as that of a minority, as long as he does not instruct people to act in accordance with that view. In actual fact, we are not aware of any time that a person was convicted of this offense.

One of the greatest "rebels" of all times was Elisha ben Avuiah (known as Aher). He was not sentenced to death, probably because after he had apostasized he no longer taught his Torah in public, and did not issue either actual or theoretical rulings. But everyone banned and excommunicated him, scorned him and no longer mentioned his name — except for his student, R' Meir, who remained loyal to him and did not turn his back on him until the day of his death. And how does one explain that one of the greatest rabbinic authorities became a heretic? The aggadah talks of "four who entered the orchard," one of these being Elisha ben Avuiah. According to the commentators, the "orchard" is the Heavens; there are those who say the four actually ascended there, while others say they merely imagined that they had ascended. If one takes it literally, an "orchard" is a place where trees bloom, and where the smell can be positively intoxicating. There is no one who doubts that they violated the injunction of Ben Sira: "Do not seek that which is beyond you, and do not investigate that which is hidden from you; study that which you were permitted; you have no business with that which is concealed."

Thus we learn: "One who studies four things, it would have been better for him had he not been born: what is above, what is below, what is in front, and what is behind." And indeed, one of those who entered the "orchard" "looked and died"; one "looked and was harmed" (as *Rashi* explains it, he became insane); one (R' Akiva) came out whole; while Elisha ben Avuiah "cut the plants." He assumedly did not "cut the plants" of the orchard itself, because he had been intoxicated by it; one must therefore understand that his "cutting of the plants" referred to his cutting down or destroying the plants outside the orchard — and this was the Torah life that God "planted within us." This teaches us that one who enters the orchard of secular wisdom or metaphysics or other divine temptations, does so at his own risk. It is better, so they advise him, not to do so but to remain within the four cubits of the Jewish law and to take refuge with the Divine Presence. Among the sayings of Elisha that have been preserved — and they were preserved because after he had "cut the plants" the Sages had not burned or hidden them — is one which explains the words of Job, "Gold and crystal cannot equal it: and the exchange of it jewels of fine gold." "Gold" refers to the Torah, which like that metal, remains forever; whereas crystal, "once it is broken, cannot be repaired." There are those who prefer gold houses whose walls can withstand any wind; and there are those who prefer walls of glass, for even though fragile, they are transparent and are open to the light of the sun.

"Excommunication" became the most common form of punishment for the spreading of wrong views in public. If one sometimes gets the impression that this device was used too often, one should remember that they used no other punishment. Maimonides lists 24 reasons for which the court has the right to excommunicate a person, including a number which relate to freedom of speech: one who derides Torah sages (even after their deaths), one who derides an agent of the court, one who calls his fellow a slave, one who uses God's name in vain, one who take a pointless oath (e.g., to swear at noon that it is daytime), and one who excommunicates a person who does not deserve that punishment. As excommunication is made upon the declaration of a Torah scholar or scholars and as there is no requirement of investigation and judgment, there was always the danger that it would be used too freely or without sufficient deliberation. Indeed, Maimonides praises "the early righteous ones" and "great scholars" who "never excommunicated a person": "And that is the way of Torah sages that it is worth emulating," at least when the sin was not committed in public.

Excommunication because of the expressing of a minority opinion was not only the lot of R' Eleazar. We have learned:

> Akabia ben Mehalalel testified to four matters. They said to him, "Akabia, retract these four things that you said, and we will make you the head of the court of Israel." He said to them: "It is better for me to be called a fool all my life, and not to become a wicked person for an instant before God, that they should not say, 'He retracted in order to obtain a position of power.'"... They excommunicate? him and he died excommunicated. The court then stoned his coffin. R' Judah said: "Heaven forbid that Akabia was excommunicated, because no person surpassed Akabia ben Mehalalel in wisdom and fear of sin. Whom did they excommunicate? Eleazar ben Hanokh ..."

R' Judah lived four or more generations after Akabia, and he took it for granted that a righteous man such as Akabia would not be excommunicated. There was, however, a rumor or a tradition that one of the sages of that generation had been excommunicated, and they found that Eleazar ben Hanokh, of whom we know nothing else, had been excommunicated. It is said that he was excommunicated because "he questioned (the need for) cleansing the hands": the same attitude toward this tradition would later be expressed by Jesus. In the end, though, Akabia recanted on these four issues, for then there was no one who would suspect him of trying to gain authority. When his sons asked him why he had not retracted publicly earlier, he told them that his view had been adopted by him the same way the view of the majority had been adopted by it: "I heard from the majority, and they heard from the majority; I remained with what I had heard, and they remained with what they had heard"; but now that the majority had decided against him and his sons had only heard his view from him, that being the opinion of an individual, "it is proper to forsake the words of the individual and to accept the words of the majority."

XII.

The Right of Freedom

I commenced with the right to life as opposed to the punishment of death, and I will conclude with the right to freedom as opposed to the punishment of imprisonment. The "freedom" to which I am alluding is the freedom of the person to move freely — and it is a human right no less important than spiritual freedom.

There is no ancient legal system which did not include provisions for imprisonment — except for the Biblical system, which recognizes three types of punishment: death, lashes and fines, but does not recognize imprisonment as a legal punishment. As to what the other ancient systems did, the Bible gives us ample evidence.

In Egypt there was a prison, "where the prisoners of the king were imprisoned," which was administered by "the officer of the prison." Joseph was imprisoned in it, and later those in charge of the king's baked goods and of his wine were also sent there, after they had aroused the king's anger. But there were also prisoners of the poor classes, and the tenth plague, the slaying of the firstborn, affected them all, "from the firstborn of Pharaoh who sat on his throne to the firstborn of captivity who was in the pit."

As far as the Philistines are concerned, we are told that they took Samson to Gaza, where "they bound him with fetters of brass; and he ground in the prison house." The king of Assyria imprisoned Hosea the king of Israel, "and he bound him in the prison." And among the common punishments in Persia — and which the king of Persia authorized Ezra to use in Eretz Israel — was that of imprisonment.

Before returning to Ezra, let us cast a glance at the kings of Judea and Israel: Ahab had a "prison," where he put Michaiahu, "and he fed him bread of affliction and water of affliction." Zedekiah also had a "prison," where the prophet Elijah was eventually imprisoned: "And they smote him, and put him in prison in the house of Jonathan the scribe; for they had made that the prison." Later, Jeremiah was imprisoned in "the court of the prison" and in the dungeon in "the court of the prison, "there was no water, but mire; so Jeremiah sank in the mire." Afterwards he was taken out of the dungeon and returned to "the court of the prison." And the prison of Asa, king of Judea, was known as the *beit ha-mehapekhet.*

Rather than rejecting out of hand the cruelty of the kings of Judea and Israel who had acted in this as the gentile kings had acted, Maimonides deduces from the Biblical accounts that "a king of Israel has the right to imprison and to lash people to maintain respect for him" (just as Maimonides deduces from the acts of murder that took place in the days of these kings that a king of Israel has the right to kill). But there is a major principle in law, that one can never invoke a right or authority upon patently evil acts one has done: the prisons of these kings were but a means for illegal persecution and oppression, and cannot serve as proof whatsoever for any authority to imprison people. (This does not mean that a tyrannical king needs legal authority to kill or to imprison people.)

The first time that the idea of punishment by imprisonment was accepted as part of our legal code was at the time of Ezra the Scribe or shortly thereafter. We have already mentioned that Ezra was authorized by the king of Persia to imprison people. It is possible that, at the time of Ezra, there were still prisons left over from the monarchical era, and they might even have added to them, as, for example, in the words of a late prophet, "the pit wherein there is no water" from which "the prisoners of hope" were sent; and Ezra may conceivably have agreed to the opening of prisons so as to have his courts use them. According to the information in our hands, the courts did not use them, neither in the days of Ezra nor thereafter. Ezra's agreement, though, did not remain merely a historic

111

curiosity, for the sages of the Talmud saw to include this institution in the oral law. A law of various idolatrous countries, one taken clearly from the non-Jews, a punitive authority that was borrowed from the royal courts of idolaters and which was infamous for its cruelty, entered the Jewish stream, was "naturalized" in our legal system, and became a source for punitive authority by the Jewish courts.

This does not mean that there hadn't arisen in earlier times the need to incarcerate suspects, lest they run away from the courts: already in the Torah we are told that they placed the man who had blasphemed "under guard, because it had not been explained what should be done to him." Until God would reveal to them the man's fate, they placed him under guard. And the same thing happened with the man who had chopped wood on the Sabbath day. When Joseph's brothers were suspected of stealing his goblet, he prevented them from travelling and placed them "under guard" — not in Pharaoh's prison, but in a house or houses that were guarded continuously. After the Sages authorized imprisonment, they interpreted the references to "under guard" in the Torah as imprisonment: "This teaches us that all those who are guilty of capital crimes are imprisoned." Indeed that was the way they acted and they ruled the law to be, but the Torah statement of "under guard" does not have to mean that.

There were sages that were very concerned about the imprisoning of a person only because he was suspected of having committed a crime. They asked: "Does that mean that one sentences a person when there is a doubt?" Until the person is declared guilty in an authorized court, he should enjoy the benefit of the doubt, and should not be imprisoned while there is still doubt as to his guilt. To this they answered: "What then should we do? A certain person killed a man, and is he to run around free until he is sentenced?" R' Jose asked: "Is a person then to be seized in the market and humiliated?" They thereupon decided that no person was to be imprisoned until "the two witnesses had arrived against him" — today we would say, until there is a *prima facie* case against him. Similarly, they ruled that if a person argues with another and injures him seriously and we do not know if the person will recover or will die of his wound, the person who injured him is imprisoned until things become clear: "Can you imagine that this one will walk about in the market place while the other was killed? This teaches that they imprison him, and if the person dies, they kill him" — in other words, he is put on trial for murder.

We have already seen, in discussing the death penalty, the great difficulties the Sages imposed in the implementation of this punishment — until they effectively removed the possibility of implementing it totally. But how does one allow a person who has killed another "to work outside" and possibly endanger society as a whole? Imprisonment, then, is the simplest way to restrain a person's movements and deeds. Therefore the Mishnah states: "One who kills a person without witnesses is placed in confinement and is fed poor bread and water of oppression." The same is true for recidivists: if a person is supposed to receive a lashing for having violated a law for which the penalty is *karet*, and if he has already been lashed three times for violating that law, "the court sends him to prison and they feed him barley until his belly bursts." As to a person who killed another "without witnesses," this refers to a murderer where the evidence against him is not enough to convict him in accordance with the law but where there is no doubt whatsoever about his guilt; for example, if there was only one eyewitness rather than two; or if there were only witnesses who saw the murder but not witnesses to warn the murderer before the act itself; or if there was only circumstantial evidence, but enough that left no doubt as to the man's guilt. A murderer was not put on trial unless there was sufficient testimony against him to convict him in accordance with the law. And if all of this evidence existed and the murderer was put on trial, the court could still declare him innocent because of contradictions in the testimony of the witnesses. One who is not convicted by the court cannot be punished; and one who is convicted must, by Torah law, be punished by being put to death by the court and by no other means. Thus we see that the placing of the murderer under guard was not a punishment, but was an administrative procedure to protect the public welfare.

113

It is not as if the murderer cared whether he was being imprisoned as punishment or in order to protect the public; only from a theoretical point of view is there significance to the fact that the sages of the Talmud did not claim to add the punishment of incarceration to the punishments listed in the Torah: even after Ezra's era, imprisonment served administrative purposes and not judicial aims.

The difference between "poor bread and water of oppression" on the one hand, and "barley," on the other, is that one is able to subsist on bread and water, whereas in the case of "barley," he was fed "until his stomach burst" — and the reason for this, evidently, was that those who were obligated to be lashed had been lawfully convicted, and had it not been for the kindness of the Sages in permitting lashes instead of *karet*, they would have deserved *karet* for their first sin. It is not that the Sages claimed to be carrying out the punishment of *karet*, which is a divine prerogative, but they allowed God to see to it that the "barley" would bring about its natural effects. (There is a view that both are to be fed "poor bread and water of oppression," and afterwards "barley until their stomachs burst" — and even though Maimonides ruled in accordance with this view, this interpretation does not fit into the language of the Mishnah.)

According to the *Tosefta*, if a person was warned four times and he did not even listen to the fourth warning, he was placed in confinement. Here he had not yet committed any sin, and he was imprisoned only to prevent him from sinning in the future. Of two possible evils, that of murder on the one hand and that of imprisonment on the other, one chooses the lesser of the two.

R' Judah said that the prison cell must be "the height of a man" — and this, evidently, was the minimum demand, because the pits they used in those days (and as late as in the medieval era), did not permit a person to stand up straight.

But we do not hear that anyone was every placed in such a confined space. On the other hand, we hear a great deal about individuals that were placed in prison — and these, according to all the signs, were the Roman prisons that the occupiers set up in the country (or they, too, may have been left-over monarchical prisons predating the destruction of the Temple). To the Talmudic sages, there was nothing worse than being incarcerated in a prison, and they raised "the ransoming of captives" to the level of a holy commandment, or, in their language, to "a great commandment." But "one does not ransom captives above their value, because of the stability of the world" — one does not pay more than is customary, because otherwise the world won't be able to survive the inflated prices. So too, one does "not smuggle out captives," either for "the stability of the world" or because of "the decree of the captives" — the "stability of the world" means so that their captors should not wreak vengeance on future captives, while "the decree of the captives" refers to the concern that their captors may take vengeance on the captives they still hold, because one of these was smuggled out. Aiding a captive to escape is considered to be a form of "redemption," and especially as it is known that "a person in captivity cannot free himself from prison," without help from the outside.

The day a man is released from prison is a holiday. Even an idolater makes a party for his son on the day "that he leaves the prison." A slave who has succeeded in fleeing from his prison goes free, and one forces his owner to sign a bill of release. If a prisoner is released on one of the intermediate days of the festivals he may shave, even though others are forbidden to do so on that day. Samuel the Lesser says if a child is born to a person on a day that one is forbidden to cut one's hair and the quantity of hair on his head is oppressive, "he is permitted to cut his hair on the intermediate day, for one does not have a bigger prison than that."

The Sages made sure not to use anything that might be construed to be a prison; the place that the high priest was sequestered for seven days before the Day of Atonement was referred to as a *dirah* — a "residence" — "A residence against one's will is also called a residence, so that they should not say that the high priest was in prison."

And they related a parable: "This is like a person who was incarcerated in a prison. They said to him: 'We will release you tomorrow and give you a large sum of money.' He answered them: 'Release me today, and I ask for nothing.'"

It is superfluous to mention that a person who is freed from prison recites the *ha-gomel* blessing praising God for His goodness, for being freed is a mercy of God, as it states: "The Lord frees the imprisoned, the Lord opens the eyes of the blind, the Lord straightens those who are bent."

Even according to those who hold that imprisonment is a permissible and desirable means of punishment, as Maimonides, one is forbidden to deprive a person of his freedom in excess of what is necessary:

> The judge may ... imprison a person in prison ... to the extent that he sees the person deserves it and the times dictate so — and in everything his (i.e., the judge's) deeds should be for the sake of heaven, and respect for his fellow-man should not be unimportant to him.

We have seen that a person who cannot pay his debts may sell himself into slavery, and that one who stole can be sold by the court. But a creditor cannot demand that a person be imprisoned, and the court is not permitted to imprison him. Of slavery and imprisonment, slavery is the lesser evil. A slave, too, is free to move about and to breathe fresh air and enjoy the sun, but whoever was imprisoned in those days never left the prison cell and had nothing. In many legal systems, including that of Israel today, people are imprisoned for failure to pay debts, if they have no assets to pay these debts; and in Jewish communities of the Middle Ages as well they emulated the non-Jewish legal systems and imprisoned people for failure to pay their debts. But the Torah law is not like that. In the language of Maimonides:

> By Torah law, when a creditor demands payment of the debt owed him, if the debtor has assets, one ensures that he retains the minimum necessary and gives the rest to the creditor ... and if the debtor has nothing, or he only has the bare minimum, the debtor goes about unmolested, and he is not imprisoned, and one does not say to him: "Bring proof that you are poor."

This statement by Maimonides is based on what the Torah states:

"If you lend money to My people, the poor who is with you, you shall not be with him as an usurer" — and the words "the poor who is with you" are interpreted as meaning, "Consider as if you yourself were poor" (*Rashi*). The Sages went even further and stated that not only is the creditor forbidden to apply the strict letter of the law in his efforts to regain his money, but he is even forbidden "to walk past" his debtor, so that the latter should not be embarrassed.

Much more dangerous than creditors were the "redeemers of blood"; while the former pursued a person in order to exact payment, the latter pursued a person to kill him after he had killed the latter's relatives. Whereas the danger from the former was servitude and the loss of freedom, the danger from the latter was the loss of one's life. In order to protect the person who had killed through negligence from the redeemer of blood, the Torah commanded the Israelites to establish "cities of refuge." As long as the killer was within one of these cities, the redeemer of blood could not touch him. If the redeemer of blood claimed that the killing was not an act of negligence but was done deliberately, he had to accuse the killer before the courts and had to prove his allegations with clear evidence. If he succeeded in proving his case, the person was sentenced as any murderer, whereas if the redeemer of blood did not succeed in proving his case, the killer was returned to the city of refuge. Even in this city of refuge, which was meant to protect the killer through negligence from the (natural, and by Torah law, legitimate) lust for revenge of those who pursued him, there was a deprivation of freedom of movement — and it is therefore of interest to see how the sages of the Talmud lessened the severity of this deprivation. The Torah states: "He shall flee to one of these cities and live," which, taken literally, implies that by residing in one of these cities, the person's life is saved. The Sages, though, explained that this means that the person had to be provided with a way to earn a living and support himself, and he only had to work in his own occupation: even "if a rabbi is exiled, his yeshivah is exiled with him." A certain number of occupations, which were considered to be dangerous, were not permitted in the cities of refuge: "One does not lay traps in them, one does not stretch ropes across in them, and one does not sell weapons in them." In order for life there to be as pleasant as possible, it was determined that these cities of refuge should not be small villages nor large cities, but "medium-sized cities"; that they should only be established where water was plentiful; and the sages had to ensure that within the permanent population of the city would be "Priests, Levites and Israelites." Accommodations in the cities of refuge were free, in houses established for this purpose by the authorities (when refuge was also offered in the cities of the Levites in addition to the six cities of refuge stated in the Torah, they charged a rental fee, but not in the cities of refuge). Once a person who had killed another reached a city of refuge, "he would stand at the gate to the city and would tell the elders of the city his account, and they would allow him to enter the city and give him a place to stay, where he would reside with them." Whoever fled to a city of refuge remained there "until the death of the high priest, and after the death of the high priest the killer could return to his own place." Even if the high priest died shortly after the killer had been admitted to the city of refuge, in which case the killer's confinement was of very short duration, should the redeemer of blood kill him, he would be guilty of murder. On the other hand, should the killer leave the city of refuge before the death of the high priest, or if he had never fled to it, and the redeemer of blood killed him, the latter could not be convicted, because he had not committed any crime.

There are no longer "redeemers of blood" in the world. No person decides the law for himself or executes it by himself — and if he does so, he will have to pay the consequences. But the moral lesson that the Torah gave us still remains true today: if a person's freedom must be denied for the protection of the public, it would be best that the imprisonment not be punitive but a humanitarian refuge.